GEORGE WILLIAMS AND THE Y.M.C.A.

George Williams and the Y.M.C.A.

A study in Victorian social attitudes

CLYDE BINFIELD

HEINEMANN : LONDON

William Heinemann Ltd
15 Queen St, Mayfair, London W1X 8BE

LONDON   MELBOURNE   TORONTO
JOHANNESBURG   AUCKLAND

920

434   07090   4

Printed in Great Britain by
Cox & Wyman Ltd
London, Fakenham and Reading

This book is lovingly dedicated

to my wife

who was prepared to encounter George
Williams even on honeymoon. It was a
brief encounter, since Williams had a
profound belief in marriage.

Contents

Illustrations

A map of *George Williams's London* precedes Part I.

Preface

If a book is called a 'Life and Times' it is usually because there is insufficient material for a 'Life'. This is such a book. It is easier to say what it is not. It is not a biography. J. E. Hodder Williams wrote that with great verve, and little new material has since appeared. It is not a history of the British Y.M.C.A., although such a book is greatly needed, and any study of George Williams is quickly enveloped in the Association which he founded. It is not a history of the World's Alliance, although George Williams wielded great influence throughout the movement. C. P. Shedd's work remains the standard history of that.

In fact it really does try to be a 'Life and Times'. No history is free of the prejudices of its writer; no history, indeed, can be definitive. George Williams is sufficiently remarkable to merit reappraisal according to the prejudices of the late twentieth century. His life as a businessman and a philanthropist is instructive; his life as a Christian is all-important. Above all he is representative of people who are known about but seldom written about: they are taken for granted. His sort of times are important: the shop assistants' world of the 1840s, the world of benevolent societies, and Nonconformist ministers; the world of the great philanthropists; the world of Low Churchmen of the Portman Chapel type. From this world grew the Y.M.C.A. which is again surprisingly taken for granted.

He was not, strictly speaking, the founder of the Y.M.C.A. There were many founders, and not enough note has been taken of men like David Nasmith. But it is convenient to call him the founder, and not really incorrect. He and the Y.M.C.A. were identified for over sixty years. Yet the Y.M.C.A. developed an outlook far beyond his, even during his lifetime. Its attitudes to politics, education, recreation, let alone the ecumenical implications of an Evangelical Christian faith, developed in ways which could not have been foreseen. These developments are part of Williams's life; he did not exactly grow with them, but he never repudiated the Y.M.C.A., and at stages in its growth he played a crucial part in the decisions which made its wider growth possible.

The reasons for this are complex. Some lie in his character – he was a good judge of men, he was frank and manly, those under-valued Victorian qualities. Some lie in what was happening to his faith through agencies like the Moody campaigns, or Keswick. Some lie in his family: he learned from experience, and he was sentimental enough to cherish the most distant links. The Hitchcocks and Williamses were numerous enough. Perhaps they could not have been more ordinary, yet the clan and its connexions produced a leading wholesaler (George Williams), two publishers of genius (Matthew Hodder and J. E. Hodder Williams) and the pioneer of convenient travel (Thomas Cook). They settled in Australia, New Zealand, and South Africa as well as Bromley and Upper Norwood; from a host of Anglican clergymen and Free Church missionaries they produced a Dean (of Manchester) and an Archbishop (of the West Indies). More recent descendants have ventured into politics. In its way this was a world as distinctive, and as far reaching in its implica-tions, as that of Noel Annan's 'intellectual aristocracy' of the same cen-tury or of Lewis Namier's parliamentary cousinhood of the previous century. This became George Williams's world, which is why a 'Life and Times' might be justified, for all the stools it falls between.

I owe a profound debt to the help of a great many people. Without exception their response has been generous and courteous, and I hope that they will not feel that they have been repaid discourteously, by relegation to an alphabetical list. Each name represents much more than conventional thanks. None must be considered responsible for any errors of fact or variation of interpretation which may be found in the narrative.

I must, however, acknowledge four especial debts: to Geoffrey F. Palmer, of the National Council of Y.M.C.As. who introduced me to George Williams; to G. Ronald Howe, of the National Council of Y.M.C.As., whose resourcefulness in uncovering material and enthusiasm in upholding the work were limitless; to the adminis-trators of the Sheffield University Research Fund, which made possible much of my work on George Williams; and to Professor John Roach who read the typescript and from whose tactful sugges-tions I have greatly benefited.

I am indebted to the following: Mr L. H. Adams (London Central

Y.M.C.A.); Mrs. A. Adburgham; Mr. J. Attenborough; Mr. W. T. Authers; Mrs. P. Baker (Librarian, Wood County District Public Library, Bowling Green, Ohio); Revd. H. L. Bevan; Mr. W. E. Bigglestone (Archivist, Oberlin College); Mrs. J. C. G. Binfield; Miss M. Boase; Revd. Dr. R. Brown; Mrs. M. Carotenuto; Mr. R. J. Carwardine; Revd. A. J. Coates; Mr. I. P. Collis (Archivist, Somerset Record Office); Revd. D. H. Cummins; Miss E. M. Davies; Mr. A. Dunn (Bridgwater Borough Librarian); Mr. R. A. G. Dupuis; Mr. P. J. Edwards, Mr. C. A. Elliott (Chief Librarian, Islington Public Library); Dr. R. J. M. Evans; Miss I. M. Fletcher (Librarian and Archivist, Livingstone House, London); Mr. C. J. Gibling; Mr. F. Gilbert; Miss J. Gilbert (Assistant Archivist, Methodist Archives); Miss K. E. Goodfellow; Mr. P. Grail; Dr. W. N. Gunson; Mr. A. J. M. Henstock (Acting Archivist, Nottinghamshire Record Office); Revd. D. J. Hillier; Miss J. Hofmann (Assistant Archivist, Dorset Record Office); Mr. G. E. Hoskin; Mrs. J. Howarth; Mr. H. G. Hughes; Mr. E. J. Hunt; Revd. T. Illingworth Jagger; Mr. J. H. Jamieson; Mrs. S. Johnson; Mr. P. A. Kennedy (Archivist, Devon Record Office); Mr. P. I. King (Archivist, Northamptonshire Record Office); Dr. G. Kitson Clark; Professor Kupisch; Mr. J. Lello; Mr. N. McGill (Chief Librarian, Mansfield Public Library); Mrs. E. M. Mead; Mr. R. E. Mutter; Miss L. Penrose; Mr. T. W. Pike; Revd. J. C. Pollock; Mr. N. S. E. Pugsley (Exeter City Librarian); Mr. A. H. S. Reid; the late Mr. J. Rider Smith; Revd. E. E. Sadler; Mr. E. H. Sargeant (Archivist, Worcestershire Record Office); Mrs. E. Gordon Selwyn; Miss L. M. Sieveking; Mr. B. S. Smith (Archivist, Gloucestershire Record Office); Mr. J. Smith; Revd. G. Snell; Mr. P. A. Snow; Revd. J. M. Stanton; Revd. R. Taylor; Revd. K. Twinn (Librarian, Dr. Williams's Library); Mr. B. Underwood; Mr. P. H. Valantine; Mr. A. H. Watkins (Bromley Borough Librarian); Mr. J. P. Wells (Oxford City Librarian); Mr. H. G. Wheeler; Revd. D. M. Whyte; Mr. G. Wickens; Mr. J. Wigley; Mr. H. Williams; Mr. K. C. Williams; Mr. P. Wright.

For supplying and for giving me permission to use illustrations I have pleasure in acknowledging the kindness of the following:

The National Council of Y.M.C.As. (Plates 1; 4 – Morley, Shaftesbury; 5; 6).

Hodder & Stoughton Ltd., publishers of J. E. Hodder Williams's *The Life of Sir George Williams* (Plates 2*a*; 2*b*; 8*b*).

The Greater London Council Print Collection (Plates 3*b*; 7*b*; 8*a*).
Dr. Williams's Library (Plate 4 – Binney, Leifchild).

I must also express my appreciation to Miss R. Wells of Sheffield
University Library, whose diligence at Inter-Library Loan was sorely
tested, and to Mrs. P. C. Holland and Miss H. M. Pack, whose
Christian forbearance grew rapidly when confronted with my hand-
writing.

Sheffield   CLYDE BINFIELD

Abbreviations

The following abbreviations are used in the text and in references:

C.I.M.   China Inland Mission
C.V.J.M.   Christlicher Verein Junger Männer
D.N.B.   Dictionary of National Biography
Johnson Cuttings Scrapbook of newspaper cuttings in the possession of Mrs. S. Johnson
L.M.S.   London Missionary Society
Nat.Counc.Mss.   Material in the keeping of the National Council of Y.M.C.As.
P.S.A.   Pleasant Sunday Afternoons
Selwyn Cuttings   Scrapbook of newspaper cuttings in the possession of Mrs. B. Gordon Selwyn
U.Y.M.C.A.   Glasgow United Young Men's Christian Association
W.M.L.D.R.A.   Working Men's Lord's Day Rest Association
Y.M.C.A.   Young Men's Christian Association
Y.W.C.A.   Young Women's Christian Association
Y.M.S.R.I.   Glasgow Young Men's Society for Religious Improvement

The Hitchcock Family
The Williams Family

Relationships are shown in the charts
which begin overleaf
and these are followed by
a map of
George Williams's London

The Hitchcock Family

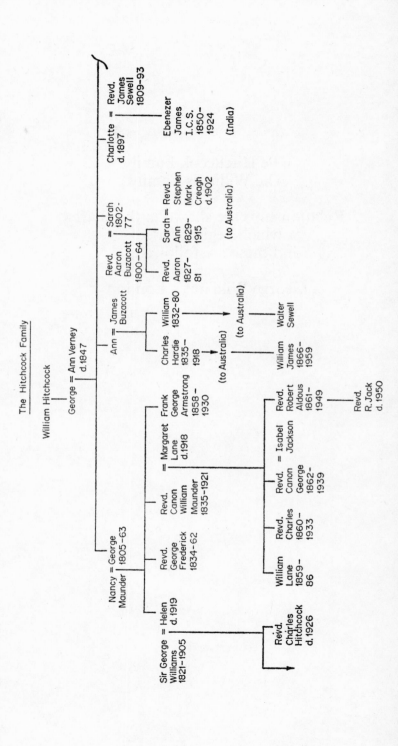

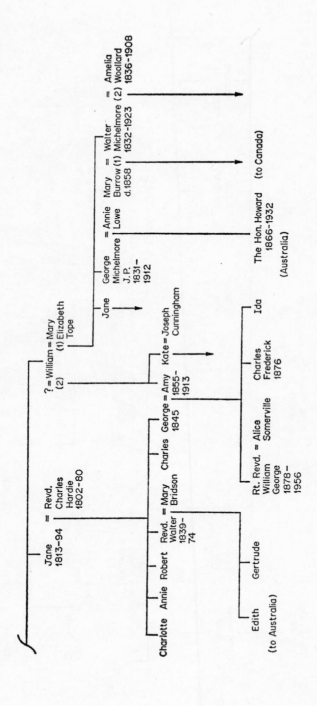

Jane
1813–94

? = William = Mary
      (1)   Elizabeth
      (2)   Tope

Jane →

George
Michelmore
J.P.
1831–
1912

= Annie
  Lowe

Mary = Walter
Burrow (1) Michelmore
d.1858   1832–1923

(to Canada)

= Amelia
  Woollard
  1836–1908

The Hon. Howard
1866–1932

(Australia)

Jane = Revd.
1813–94 Charles
         Hardie
         1802–80

Charlotte Annie Robert Revd. = Mary   Charles George = Amy
                          Walter Bridson   1845   1855–
                          1839–   1913
                          74

Kate = Joseph
       Cunningham
       →

Edith
(to Australia)

Gertrude

Rt. Revd. = Alice
William   Somerville
George
1878–
1956

Charles
Frederick
1876

Ida

The Williams Family

Amos Williams = Ann Betty —
d. 1841

Charles 1819–1900	William Frederick b. 1813	John 1807–90 →	Richard c. 1814–69 →

Sir George = Helen Hitchcock
1821–1905   d. 1919

Thomas Cook 1808–92

John Mason d. 1899

Nancie = Albert 1862–1941
(1)

Barbara Crowe
(2)

Jane Mary = Sir Francis Portal Bt.

Helen

Alfred = Rose Thomas Gibbs d. 1908

Revd. = Ellen Mary Charles Sibthorpe Hitchcock d. 1926 d. 1926

Howard = Lily Delves d. 1929

Frederick = Blanche George Dannatt 1855– d. 1941 1938

Cicely   Gordon   George   Hugh   Leslie

Stanley = Marie Louise de Pfeffel →

Colin   Ashley   2 daughters →

Capt. = Eric Smith

11th = Fortune Duke of Grafton

John D.L., M.P.

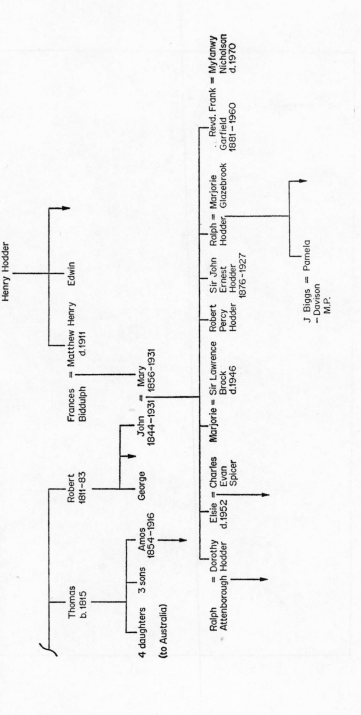

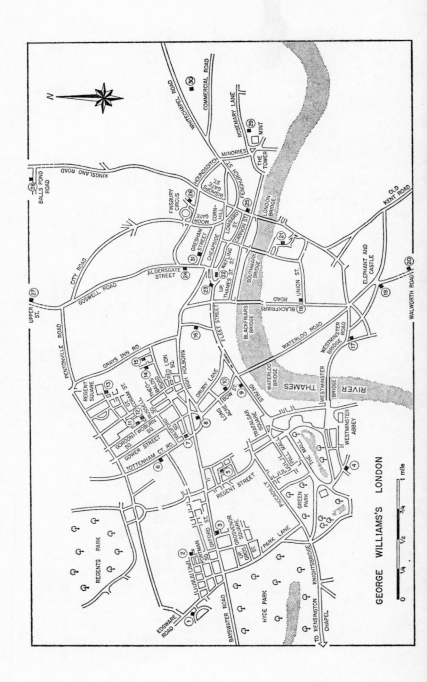

GEORGE WILLIAMS'S LONDON

This is an over-simplified map of a city which changed with frightening rapidity between 1837 and 1901. It will be appreciated that in the earlier part of this period Charing Cross Road and Shaftesbury Avenue did not exist; Pimlico, Belgravia, Bayswater and sections of Islington were still largely rural; if it was already clear that if the near future lay with the Suburban chapels, the present was still solidly with those in the City; and all were within walking distance for a healthy young man. By the end of the period London was the imperial city which it remained until recently.

1. George Hitchcock's house, Norfolk Crescent.
2. Portman Chapel, Portman Square.
3. The new King's Weigh House Chapel, Duke Street.
4. Westminster Chapel, Buckingham Gate.
5. Craven Chapel, Foubert's Place.
6. Whitefield's, Tottenham Court Road.
7. London Central Y.M.C.A., Tottenham Court Road.
8. Bloomsbury Baptist Chapel.
9. Exeter Hall, Strand.
10. Crown Court Church of Scotland.
11. The Williams house, Woburn Square.
12. The Williams house, Russell Square.
13. Regent Square Presbyterian Church.
14. St. John's, Bedford Row.
15. John St. Baptist Chapel.
16. Fetter Lane Chapel.

17. Christ Church Westminster Bridge Road.
18. Surrey Chapel.
19. The Metropolitan Tabernacle.
20. York St. Chapel, Walworth.
21. New Park St. Chapel.
22. St. Paul's Cathedral.
23. 72–74 St. Paul's Churchyard.
24. London Central Y.M.C.A., 165 Aldersgate Street.
25. The old King's Weigh House Chapel, Fish Street Hill.
26. The Hitchcock house, Blomfield St.
27. Union Chapel, Islington.
28. Maberley Chapel, Kingsland.
29. The Darby St. Mission.
30. Wycliffe Chapel.
31. London Y.M.C.A., Gresham Street buildings.

BOOK I

An Apprenticeship in the Best of Both Worlds

CHAPTER I

'The Y.M.C.A. has been jubileeing'

Early in 1908 when there was question of revising the official *Life*
J. E. Hodder Williams, Sir George's grand-nephew and biographer,
wrote amiably to W. H. Mills:

> 'The fact is that when once the book was done I thankfully tied
> up everything I had into one big bundle, and I hope never to open
> it as long as I live ... The very sight of its cover alone makes me
> ill ... You had better put on a man whose moral character you
> do not think will be completely wrecked by the effort.'[1]

Ernest Hodder Williams was a young man of great moral character
and exciting business sense. He was also a very busy man and destined
not to be long-lived. So it is easy to sympathize with his rather
desperate refusal. The writing of an official biography is an honour-
able but delicate task. Convention demands too many omissions and
the Williams family tended to be conservative and over-correct in
such matters. There was a minimum of personal material on which
to draw. Family history, which is taken for granted by aristocrats, is
more appropriate to the professional classes or to declining gentle-
folk. Aspiring businessmen should have no time for it, and for
Evangelical Christians the examination involved is an irrelevance
unless it is religious. Most of the Williams family were evangelically-
inclined businessmen. Yet there must be a 'Life'. George Williams
was, after all, the founder and the ideal of an international movement. He had become a legend long before his death, and if sophisticated people now felt that he belonged to a long-past generation, at
least he had the fortune to die at a time when most still yearned for
simple tales of faith and pertinacity and their rewards.

Even Edwardian England craved heroes and George Williams was a hero. He was buried in St. Paul's Cathedral, and there is a window to him in Westminster Abbey. There is also a bust of him in Taunton Shire Hall and one in the vestibule of Dominant House, the head-quarters of Hitchcock, Williams and Co. There are portraits of him in Dulverton where he is still regarded as a local boy. The Central Y.M.C.A. in London is prolific in relics – his glasses, his cradle, his Bible, his desk, his Freedom Casket. In the lands of the free he is commemorated by two universities. In London there is an annual lecture.

Yet he is little known to the general public and to his own move-ment he is unreal – wholly admirable, a trifle improbable, and truth to tell a shade uncomfortable. The business man was rather too easily transformed into the perfect knight – the memorial window in the Abbey is very knightly. The young man became rather too firmly a father figure – the busts and the portraits are very patriarchal. There is a simplicity in this image which is not appealing to later genera-tions, and it is not easy to explain.

The dilemma which confronted Hodder Williams still faces his fellow biographers. Hodder Williams was presented with few per-sonal papers, many Annual Reports, and pursued with a mass of delightful reminiscences. As befitted a man whose company published thrilling yarns as well as theological works, he was keenly aware of his public. The result was a period piece, informative where least expected, immensely readable and immensely annoying, because however much George Williams's life needs to be reinterpreted, the materials for this remain inadequate. His biographers are doomed in their turn to write period pieces and their subject deserves more than that.

It is possible to convey this difficulty – the simplicity of the story hiding undercurrents which could not have been absent – by describ-ing the celebrations of 1894. The last decade of Williams's life became one long jubilee. It could not have been otherwise. The concerns to which he had devoted his life – his family, his business, his movement and his faith – were flowering. His was one of the happiest success stories of the age and perhaps men sensed that it was among the last. In an England devoted to Jubilees, the Jubilee of the Y.M.C.A. in June 1894 was memorable. The Queen's Jubilee of 1887 had released the passion for commemoration which was never far from the Vic-torian heart and in the 1890s Jubilees engulfed businesses and institutions and famous men.

In 1891 Thomas Cook's travel agency took its turn. For *The Times*, Thomas Cook was 'a typical middle-class nineteenth-century Englishman', and he and his son were 'the Julius and the Augustus Caesar of modern travel'.[2] There was an imperial air about them which expressed the yearnings of Englishmen and their duties: 'they are as ubiquitous as the Flag in Mr. Kipling's poems', 'it is only the absence of a railway that prevents them from issuing tourist tickets for the moon',[3] and their jubilee dinner was graced by Royalty and the Military. As a correspondent put it writing from Hampstead:

'In reference to Messrs. Cook and Son, the excursionists, it may be of interest to some to hear what an intelligent Italian once said to me some years ago, when travelling in Italy. He said that Messrs. Cook and Son had done more to bring about the unity of the Italian nation than any military or political influence, through their introduction of the railway circular Tourist ticket....'[4]

Typical, middle-class, nineteenth-century Englishmen could have no nobler goals. Between the Cook and Williams families there was sympathy and friendship as there was between Cook's commercial organization and Williams's Christian association. Harold Begbie, seeking to popularize Williams and his work, expressed this when he spoke of 'an empire of Christian manhood', of 'a consecrated Anglo-Saxon brotherhood' and of the Y.M.C.A. becoming 'the great central labour exchange of the whole empire'.[5] What could be more providential?

For George Williams, personally, 1894 was a time of delightful providence – he was knighted. That was an honour which vindicated so many things. It recognized his personal services to London, and no Prime Minister has known more of the workings of London than Lord Rosebery, who recommended the honour; it was an accolade for the entire drapery trade, and drapers more than other tradesmen were professionally aware of social distinctions; and of course it was an acknowledgment of the worth of the Y.M.C.A. itself. That, for George Williams, was the main thing. On Tuesday, 22 May, he noted in his diary, marking the entry with three crosses as was his wont in moments of particular exaltation, 'Her Majesty the Queen, through the Prime Minister created me a Knight' and on 18 July he noted again, this time with five crosses, 'Great day at Windsor Castle. Knighted by the Queen after lunch. Kissed the Queen's hand. 20 others – several Christians....'[6]

The twenty others were typical enough of investitures. The usual politicians and businessmen included Isaac Pitman, the inventor of shorthand, Wemyss Reid, the journalist and biographer, Robert Reid, a future Lord Chancellor, and Richard Tangye, the pious Birmingham manufacturer. The Duke of York was present.[7] George Williams, the London draper, fitted in well enough with them, but it was, as he came to see, George Williams the Christian man who had been honoured and stories were told to illustrate this.

Apparently, J. H. Putterill was with Williams when the news came. 'It belongs to our Master, let us put it at His feet', and together they knelt in prayer.[8] There is also the story which is told of other men yet which is immensely illuminating. The secretary brought in the day's post, including the gracious letter. 'Have you read it?' Williams asked. 'Yes, sir'. 'Of course I shall refuse'. The secretary, who knew his George Williams, persisted: 'Might I be permitted to speak further, sir?' 'Yes, of course, go on, we're old friends.' 'Well sir, I knew you would refuse if you saw it for yourself alone – but see it for the Y.M.C.A. – as an honour for them.' 'Thank you my dear fellow – I didn't see it like that – that makes it quite different – as you go out, turn my notice round on the door – I don't wish to be disturbed, because I must lay this before the Lord.' As the secretary reached the door, Williams added, 'And no nonsense about letters to Lady Williams.'[9]

Such stories lose nothing in the telling and this one is unlikely without being improbable.

Surrounding this personal gratification were twelve months of jubilee. The world membership of the movement had reached half a million and the British celebration was the largest such function held in the country. The sermons preached in commemoration were legion, the amounts consumed at banquets phenomenal, the congregations at services and the audiences at meetings unparalleled. For the first week in June the strain and excitement were intense. Distinguished visitors poured in. 'Prince Oscar Bernadotte, with his retinue of two hundred faithful fellow-subjects', Count Bernstorff and Baron Rothkirch 'another noble German', 'Young Prince Lieven from St Petersburg'.[10]

On 1 June the Bishop of London in Westminster Abbey 'dilated on the perils and temptations that are inevitable to youth'. It continued as it had begun. George Williams appeared on the platform of Exeter Hall with two of the four surviving founder members.

There was a luncheon for 2,300 on the Thames Embankment which included 'a *recherché* sweet course and a bountiful dessert' and where the 'pop of mineral waters' drowned the clatter and the chatter. There was a reception in the Guildhall where George Williams was made a Freeman of the City of London and where 'the Swedish choir went very vigorously and effectively through a short programme . . .' while 'Messrs Coote and Tinney's band was performing in the library and the band of the Royal Artillery was stationed in the crush-rooms.' There was a vast thanksgiving in St. Paul's Cathedral and on 6 June, Jubilee Day (when the Prime Minister's horse Ladas won the Derby in a field of seven, the smallest of the century, and *The Times* congratulated the victor upon 'his first real success' as Prime Minister[11]) there was a quite remarkable gathering, part service, part party, part concert at the Royal Albert Hall. It was a day of messages and drenching rain. Tea was provided at the invitation of Louisa, Lady Ashburton. There followed a gymnastics display and 'a particularly enjoyable selection of sacred music'.

A bust of Sir George was unveiled and presented and then, amidst prolonged applause, Mme. Antoinette Sterling, with the sense of occasion peculiar to the late Victorian prima donna, 'created quite a little dramatic touch in the proceedings when, in place of an encore, which was vociferously demanded, she moved slowly up into the midst of the verdure on the platform, and in her strong clear voice said: "Dear brothers and sisters, let us have but one country – God's country; let us have but one Church – the great invisible Church; and let us love our Father, Mother, God, with all our heart and soul, and our neighbours as ourselves".'

The following day was no less memorable. The Queen had invited the delegates to visit Windsor, an invitation which had been greeted in 'curious and striking' fashion by singing the National Anthem, and on 7 June, in special trains provided by Thomas Cook and Son of Ludgate Circus, the 'Royal Homestead' was invaded. Williams rested and two of his sons took his place, leading the delegates to the mausoleum at Frogmore, accompanying them with hearty toasts 'in temperance beverages' and posing with them in an enormous photograph. 'I never saw a manlier, jollier, better behaved gathering', commented *Modern Society*, and Jerome K. Jerome added in *To-Day*, 'The Y.M.C.A. has been jubileeing. It has held meetings, spoken, sung, prayed, indulged even in the mild dissipation of a magic-lantern entertainment, and a visit to Windsor Castle.' The Queen, of course, had the last word. Her secretary, Sir Henry Ponsonby, wrote from Osborne with marvellous tact to Sir George Williams:

'I am commanded by the Queen to thank you for the magnificent Photograph you have sent to Her Majesty but I am afraid it was so late when Her Majesty saw it that she could not fully appreciate the value of this work of art.

'I hope later that the Queen will have leisure to study it more carefully.'[12]

The 1890s were an uncomfortable decade. Enthusiasm was easily transmuted into jingoism; gymnastics were too easily equated with a muscular and evangelical faith. The celebrations had been a master-piece of organization. The titled folk thronging the platforms were a tribute both to that and to the improved tone of sophisticated life. Even *The Times* newspaper which was miserly in its reporting of the Jubilee, reflected something of this when it quoted Dr. Parker's comment at a Jubilee meeting that 'the time would come when the Prime Minister of England would be an example to the young men of the Empire'.[13] A Derby victory was not to be forgiven in a Liberal Prime Minister, by young men of the 'serious and Sunday-school type'. Yet even in the breezily confident manner in which all Y.M.C.A. conferences and celebrations were described, it is impossible to ignore the undertones of a world already dominated by an armaments race and strong forces. The amity of the French and German delegations was nervously noted, and however well-intentioned Prince Lieven and Count Bernstorff were, theirs was the world of diplomacy which produced the First World War. That war tested the Y.M.C.A., and the movement emerged strengthened and able to confront a world which would have been inconceivable to George Williams. But it was the impact of that war and the next, which makes Williams and the optimism of the 1890s so alien to succeeding generations.

The events of 1914 make this quite clear. Seemingly, the hopes of the 1890s were amply fulfilled. The divisions and jealousies which had threatened to split the world's Y.M.C.As. in the early years of the twentieth century had been overcome. Membership throughout the world continued to rise. The royal patronage, so graciously extended in 1894, became more tangible. In 1907, two years after the founder's death, the Exeter Hall which throughout his adult years had epitom-ized his life as much as any building could, was demolished and from 1909 it was replaced by buildings in the Tottenham Court Road.

Ostensibly a memorial to Williams, they more accurately reflected Edwardian England. 'Wholly adequate and really magnificent'[14] they were a monument to grandeur and inadequate architecture. The precise entrance was uncertain, the rotunda wasted space without commanding respect, the general impression was of corridors and corners. It was certainly a monumental edifice: *The Daily Telegraph*, two years after its opening, kindly called it a 'splendid pile'.[15] That was on the occasion of a long awaited royal visit. The 'splendid pile', despite short notice, was decked with azaleas and cinerarias. The royal party – the Queen was looking 'remarkably well' in deep violet, with shaded marabout plumes clustered on her black velvet toque – inspected the 'splendid swimming pool' (challenging comparison with that of the Bath Club itself) and the gymnasium, where a 'series of feats of balancing exercises' caused the King to comment, 'Marvellous!' As a mark of favour and to the accompaniment of hearty cheers he allowed the large hall contained in the premises to be called King George's Hall.

This was the prelude to the movement's seventieth anniversary held this time in the Queen's Hall. The souvenir programme in gold and imitation vellum recalls a function whose pattern must by now be clear: the meeting itself, compounded of prayer, scripture, organ music and gymnastics; a royal prince in the chair, philanthropists on the platform, and messages from Archbishops and Bishops, from Woodrow Wilson and from Queen Alexandra and the Kings of Norway and Denmark.[16] Two months later in July 1914, the World's Committee of Y.M.C.As. held their plenary meetings at 13 Russell Square, the founder's old home, given by his family to be a headquarters for the National Council for England, Ireland and Wales.[17] Many of the delegates were close enough to the origins of the movement to be steeped in the evangelical single-mindedness which had characterized its founder whatever the jubilees and the 'splendid piles'. But the prayers at the Queen's Hall in 1914 were led by the Chaplain General to the Forces, and the elder statesmen meeting in Russell Square included delegates from Berlin and from St. Petersburg. Where were they four years later?

Notes

1. J. E. Hodder Williams to W. H. Mills, 27 January 1908. Nat. Counc. MSS.

2. *The Times*, 20 July 1892.
3. ibid.
4. *The Times*, 4 August 1891.
5. H. Begbie, *The Ordinary Man and the Extraordinary Thing* n.d., pp. 51, 53.
6. *Diary*, 22 May 1894; 18 July 1894.
7. *The Times*, 19 July 1894.
8. J. E. Hodder Williams, *The Life of Sir George Williams*, 1906, pp. 272–3.
9. Told to the author by Sir Frank Willis.
10. The particulars of the Jubilee came from *Association News* Special Conference Number, vol. VIII, no. 91, July 1894, *passim* esp. pp. 97–109.
11. *The Times*, 7 June 1894.
12. Letter dated 22 July 1894. Nat. Counc. MSS.
13. *The Times*, 7 June 1894.
14. Begbie, op. cit. p. 47.
15. *The Daily Telegraph*, 5 March 1914.
16. *Souvenir Programme*, 18 May 1914.
17. *Plenary Meetings of the World's Committee July 11–14 1914: Programme*.

CHAPTER II

Zion, Bridgwater, C. G. Finney, and 'the arithmetic of faith in God's arrangements'

From 1914 the life of George Williams belonged to the history of the Y.M.C.A. The world had changed too rapidly and there had been lacking that particular quality of greatness required to make such a life always relevant to men's needs, but it retained its fascination:

> 'The Y, one of humanitarianism's most heartening success stories, got started because high-strung, pint-sized George Williams was no help to his stern English farmer-father. When he upset a load of hay, his disgruntled family apprenticed him to a small-town draper. . . . A natural salesman, George Williams finally rose to ownership of his own draper's shop'.[1]

It is hard to better this succinct version of the traditional interpretation of his life.

George Williams was born on 11 October 1821, the youngest of several sons, at Ashway Farm near Dulverton on the Devon–Somerset borders. He was educated at a Dame's school in Dulverton and then at a private school in Tiverton which he left when he was 13. He worked briefly at Ashway Farm, and in 1836 he was apprenticed to a draper in Bridgwater, twenty-five miles away. Country towns were at once closer to the countryside and yet more distinct from it than is now usual and Hodder Williams has captured the significance of the move in a characteristic phrase: 'And at the journey's end was the beginning of the world.'[2]

It is tempting to portray George Williams's life as one from rags to riches. The isolation of Ashway Farm is still apparent today when the discovery of the west country as a holiday centre has tamed

Exmoor. The farmhouses of the district possess few of the refinements which their counterparts in the Home Counties might expect. To be brought up as the youngest of a large family at a time of agricultural difficulty in an area where prosperous agriculture was always uncertain, might suggest poverty or at best a certain picturesqueness. Hodder Williams, probably unconsciously, accentuated this. His publishing firm had after all made history with the English version of President Garfield's life, *From Log Cabin to White House*. Harold Begbie, with more conscious artistry, carried this to its logical conclusion contrasting the 'stalwart yeoman' father with the gentle mother, 'the angel of Ashway Farm', and the elder sons, 'tall, stark, hard-riding men, vigorous with the winds and spaces of the moorland, somewhat barbarous' with the youngest boy, diminutive, gentle and sensitive.[3]

Yet there is little direct evidence to suggest either poverty or the picturesque. The Williams family (there was apparently no connexion with Wales and later any suggestions that there might be were firmly repudiated) were long settled in the district. They were among the more solid local farmers, a position accentuated by intermarriage and suggested by Amos Williams's rather elaborate headstone in Dulverton churchyard, and they remained farmers for several generations after George Williams had removed to London. Amos Williams had been at Ashway since 1809, when he first appeared in land tax assessments for the property. Between 1810 and 1821 seven of his children were baptized at Dulverton Parish Church. Mary Ann was the eldest and the only girl, and she died nearly a year later in February 1811. The youngest, baptized on 10 December 1821, was George. In the parish register Amos was always described as 'yeoman'.[4]

George Williams's education was neither good nor systematic. Tiverton possessed two old-established schools. One, Blundells, was a grammar school in decay like many of its kind in the 1830s. The other, in Castle Street, was the Bluecoat Charity School. Williams, however, was a pupil at Gloyns's which would seem to have been a small private day school whose master, 'Old Gloyns', undertook a certain amount of extra tuition.[5] Such an education was no more than was expected of middle-class families and tradesfolk generally and rather more than the youngest son might expect. It was, moreover, of a piece with George's subsequent apprenticeship to a draper in Bridgwater.

Bridgwater was a self-contained country town of moderate size with a population of nearly 8,000. It was politically active, which meant corrupt, and for the decade after 1837 Tories represented it in parliament. Henry William Holmes, to whom George Williams was apprenticed, was the town's leading draper. His establishment had nearly thirty assistants resident on the premises. Holmes was a Dissenter and at elections he regularly supported the Whig candidates.[6] None of this suggests poverty as drapery was a progressive trade and demanded eminently personable and moderately educated assistants. It also offered tempting prospects, and a good draper was justified in demanding a high premium from his apprentices. One of the Williams boys was already in the drapery business and another, Charles, was to become a chemist. That George should follow them in trade suggests family prudence and a shrewd knowledge of their place in society.

There is, however, the story of Williams's decision to leave the farm. As Hodder Williams tells it, he caused a load of hay to be overturned just as a storm broke.[7] This not only annoyed his family, it also convinced him that God intended other things for George Williams. Another version is that Williams and his brothers were scything in the fields when Williams, reprimanded by his father for being out of line, hurled down his implement and strode from the scene.[8] The first story, which has been told to many Young Men, is in the tradition of Evangelical biography. The second is more in keeping with a normal and as yet unconverted lad.

Williams was always meticulous in maintaining links with his family and he neither disguised nor forgot his farming background. In his will he specifically mentioned all the descendants of his grandparents, paternal and maternal, and left a Bible to each one.[9] But it is from 1836, when he moved to Bridgwater, that his life developed. He was not a very imaginative adolescent and in his generation it was only the religious world which appreciated the peculiar importance of a youth's teens. At Bridgwater George Williams was converted.

In 1838 he became a committed member of a Nonconformist church. In 1839, and early in the history of the movement, he pledged himself to total abstinence. A few months after the rather sudden death of his father and after a short period helping his draper brother at North Petherton, he removed to London in the autumn of 1841, transferring his church membership to one of the leading chapels in the metropolis. His links with Bridgwater were snapping, as by 1841

his employer had ceased to live in the town and there was the prospect of the business changing hands. By now the chief influences were
working firmly on his life.

Religion was the only influence which Williams would have recognized or to which he would have attached any vital importance.
From the Sunday evening in the winter of 1837 when he sat in the
Zion Chapel at Bridgwater feeling that its minister was speaking
pointedly about his condition and that he had never realized his
condition before, he regarded himself as a committed Evangelical
Christian. Unswervingly he came to accept the Evangelical emphases
on Biblical inspiration, on eternal punishment, on a measure of predestination, on man's depravity, and on the glorious sufficiency of
the atonement. He was not a deeply reflective man and there is no
evidence that the crises of the Victorian conscience concerning these
issues ever caused his belief in them to waver. First as a Nonconformist and then for fifty years as a State Churchman he belonged
to the Evangelical party. This was of profound importance in determining the nature of the Y.M.C.A. because too often Victorian
Evangelicalism was an arid thing. The vigour of the Evangelical
Revival had lessened. The exciting developments in theological studies
and social work had passed to other schools in the Church. High
Church (which was no longer Dry Church) and Broad Church
replaced Low Church as the pace setters and Low Church could only
reply with the bitterness of ecclesiastical controversy. It produced
few statesmen among Church leaders; the most notable exception
was a layman, Lord Shaftesbury. The most vital of its standard
bearers were to be found in the Dissenting bodies and that fact alone,
with all its social and political implications, emphasized the divisions
among Evangelical Christians. It was increasingly easy for Nonconformist leaders to find common ground with the great Broad-
Churchmen rather than with the Low-Churchmen whose beliefs they
shared.

The Y.M.C.A. was among the last fruits of the Evangelical Revival.
It was not without its divisions but it retained a freshness reflecting
to a notable extent the vigour of George Williams's personal faith.
Equally important, it was a national movement regarded with
enthusiasm by Evangelical Anglicans and Evangelical Dissenters and
with approval by more moderate Churchmen. This was hardly due
to the genius of Williams but if his religious development had been
different, so would the growth of the Y.M.C.A.

It was at once the genius and the tragedy of the Evangelical insight that so much emphasis was placed on the reaction of the individual to his lot. The individual was at once a worm in the presence of God and yet, by total reliance on the merits of his Saviour, there was nothing that he could not do. To a man of sanguine and extrovert temperament like George Williams, such a belief must result in a positive, sunny faith worth more than the usual qualities of statesmanship. To the end of his life Williams held to this bracing Christian individualism with almost exasperating single-mindedness. 'Confess your sins, accept Christ, trust in Him, yield your heart to the Saviour'[10] and there is nothing a Young Man may not achieve. His message never altered and there resulted a community spirit which promised to cover the world.

There is a paradox here which the nature of Williams's first Christian allegiance might explain. On 4 February 1838 he was admitted to the fellowship of Zion Congregational Church, Bridgwater. On 14 February he was among fifteen church members attending a meeting called to revise the church rules. Beyond mention that he attended a church meeting on 2 March there is no further reference to him in the Zion minute books, though the nature of most church books is such that even this slight reference is noteworthy.[11] The point is that Church membership followed naturally upon his conversion and the duties of membership followed carefully upon enjoyment of its privileges. He was a committed Christian, which he demonstrated by becoming an Independent Dissenter.

The Williams family were Anglicans. George had been baptized into the Church of England, and although Dulverton had a Congregational Church, its buildings newly opened in 1832, there is no direct evidence to support the locally held belief that he attended its Sunday school.[12] Conscious of his own spiritual rebirth and ever afterwards a firm believer in the reality of sudden religious experience, George was painfully concerned at the seeming lack-lustre of his family's faith. The wife of his draper brother was a Unitarian[13] which was worse than indifference. Although the text on his father's tomb was impeccable: 'Jesus answered and said unto him verily verily I say unto thee except a man may be born again, he cannot see the Kingdom of God' (John III, v. 3), Williams confided to his diary his grave doubts about the seriousness of others in his large family – would that they might take it more to heart.[14] In this context membership of a Dissenting Church was the more to be noted.

Doubtless George committed himself to Zion because in Zion alone could he find vital (and respectable) religion. It was the chapel where his employer worshipped and where the Holmes establishment was expected to worship. The Congregationalism of the place was secondary. Yet while Williams was never a man to appreciate or tolerate the finer points of churchmanship, the fact remains that he became a member and not merely an adherent. At times nineteenth-century Congregationalists held loosely to their distinctive church order. Too many of their chapels were preaching-houses whose congregations knew too little of church fellowship and too much of a rather tiresome Independency. But working against this tendency was the cardinal point that Congregationalists were Nonconformists, and Nonconformists and Anglicans inhabited different worlds. The chapel might forget its fellowship, but it could never forget its social and political inferiority, and this despite its conviction of religious certainty. The man who committed himself to church membership entered an insular world, self-sufficient with its tradesfolk and even its carriagefolk, sometimes suffocating but more often exhilarating. It was impossible to be a Nonconformist without realizing what you were up against, but the challenge was great! In a country town like Bridgwater or in a glorified village like Dulverton such commitment could not be passed by, hence Mr. Holmes's attachment to the Whigs and the violence of politics in a town whose electorate was under 500.

George Williams was thus committed for under fifteen years, but those years saw him reach religious maturity and success in his business. They also saw the founding of the Y.M.C.A. No man used to a church meeting would have been ill at ease at the earlier meetings of the Y.M.C.A. No Congregationalist or Baptist would have been unduly surprised at the suspicion with which provincial associations viewed their London counterpart in later years, or at the way in which these suspicions were soothed. An Anglican or a Wesleyan Methodist might have had his reservations.

There could be little doubt about the respectability of Somerset Congregationalism. It stood firm in the tradition of the Good Old Cause and several of its Churches were of seventeenth century foundation. The Evangelical Revival had refreshed it. In 1796 a County Association was formed at South Petherton, at first for purposes of aggressive evangelism. 'You are only going to a few simple souls, tell them concerning Christ, and they will be satisfied',

Lady Huntingdon had urged two of her young men who were Somerset bound.[15]

The church in Bridgwater was formed early in the 1790s. Zion Chapel, in Friars Street, had been built in 1822.[16] Williams sat under two of its pastors and it was the first, Evan James, who had led him to Christ. James was a Welshman in his late thirties with a Welshman's regard for education and a young man's concern for his fellows. Firm in principle yet gentle in spirit he was, in Evangelical jargon, a useful pastor whose 'pulpit appeals were the means, under God, of bringing many to decision'.[17] He left Bridgwater within a year of Williams joining the fellowship, but the Evangelical has a particular regard for good men (could Williams have identified himself so completely with his movement had he not known how important one man can be in bringing another to Christ?) and in the nineteenth century world, parsons, even Nonconformist ones, held a position of the highest respectability, even in small towns. Their biographies sold readily and their portraits were reproduced in journals. No profession has since fallen so far in public esteem. It is therefore important to appreciate the influence of a man like Evan James, since to the world only actors are more quickly forgotten.

George Williams's early years as a Dissenter are usually represented as busy ones. His church was active in good works and he added to them, attending the Bible class taken by a leading member, teaching in the Sunday School and, it is said, starting a prayer meeting of his own.[18] Even his lighter moments were eminently serious. The *Morning Leader* in its obituary notice recalled his earliest known writing, a copy of the 'Dying Christian's Address to His Soul', penned in a lady's album, and signed G. W.[19] But then can a newly converted young man afford to be flippant, least of all to a lady?

Hodder Williams suggests that it was at this time that Williams was affected by the second of the religious influences in his life – an American Congregational minister named Charles Grandison Finney.[20] Finney's subsequent repute as revivalist and evangelist has been overshadowed by the later achievements of Moody and Sankey, but he was a more formidable figure and in 1838 he had reached his prime. He had recently left the Presbyterians to associate himself more firmly with the Congregationalists. At the same time Finney had left a settled pastoral ministry to connect himself with Oberlin College. For over thirty years he was pastor of the First Congregational Church, Oberlin, and from 1851 to 1866 he was president of Oberlin College itself. His fame, however, was that of a revivalist rather than a college president and it was as such that he was known in Britain. In 1849–50 and again in 1858–60, at a time of hopeful religious awakening, Finney visited the British Isles. Tall and handsome in appearance, unconventional and direct in the pulpit, he belonged to a class of pulpit orator less common among Congregationalists than among other Evangelical Christians, unafraid if at his preaching 'people burst into tears, shrieked, fainted, and fell into trances'.[21]

Finney's reputation as a writer on revivals had preceded him and was always his main source of fame in Britain. His *Sermons on Important Subjects* (1836) and *Lectures to Professing Christians* (1837), his *Skeleton of a Course of Theological Lectures* (1840) and above all his *Lectures on Revivals of Religion* were popular on both sides of the Atlantic. It is possible that Williams knew something of them while at Bridgwater. It is certain that he treasured them in London and that eventually he became personally acquainted with Finney. William Creese, the only one of the founding members to outlive Williams, considered that the glorious work which started in Hitchcock's establishment in 1844 owed most to converted young men reading *Lectures to Professing Christians* and *Lectures on Revivals of Religion* – the latter had been published in London in 1840.* Without doubt Finney's teaching illuminated truths which Williams never ceased to hold dear, but Finney is important both for the light he sheds on contemporary attitudes to revivalism and for the impetus he gave to sections of Evangelicalism which were repeatedly to influence Williams and his associates.

The 1830s was not a golden decade for Evangelical Christians.† The waves of revival which had produced the various Methodist connexions, reinvigorated the larger part of the Established Church and transformed orthodox Dissent, were now the memories of past generations. But such memories were the cause of some perplexity, particularly among the Nonconforming communities. Conversion was the sole reason for their existence; their membership depended

---

* So he told an audience at Cirencester in 1879, from an unsigned, undated *MSS History*. (? by W. H. Mills *c*. 1900) in the keeping of the National Council of Y.M.C.As.
† The following paragraph owes much to John Kent 'American Revivalism and England in the Nineteenth Century', *Papers Presented to the 'Past and Present' Conference on Popular Religion*, 7 July 1966.

upon it, even in those unevenly spaced districts where the presence since the seventeenth century of a strong and continuous Dissent had produced what was virtually a separate society – a sort of secondary Establishment. Conversion had a definite meaning for the Evangelical. It was the most intense personal experience which he expected to undergo, fraught with emotion, agony, and terrible introspection. It concerned the recognition of worthlessness and sin in the eyes of God and the need of a forgiveness which could never be deserved. If from this desolation there came an awareness that Jesus, who was God's son, had died for *you*, then you knew salvation. Your ecstasy, like your despair, was unutterable; it was also unique. For churches whose strength depended on conversion there could be no birthright membership. Consequently, the spiritual future of the children of converted parents caused a concern which was at once natural and impious, for however much you yearn for conversion, it is a gift from God. It cannot be engineered in some mechanical way. In America in the 1820s and in Britain in the 1830s this gave rise to debate. It was comforting for strong Evangelical churches if they could feel that *human* striving might, after all, contribute to the outpouring of God's grace. How else might one learn the value and power of prayer? In 1832 the Revd. Calvin Colton's *The History and Character of Revivals of Religion* argued in this way. Evangelical doctrine lent itself to academic precision and, as Colton phrased it, revivals were 'matters of human calculation, by the arithmetic of faith in God's arrangements'.[22]

Colton's book was opportune. How opportune may be gauged from the unease felt by one of London's leading Dissenting ministers. Andrew Reed, who frequently appears at the edges of George Williams's concerns, is famous for his philanthropies. He was also pastor of Wycliffe Congregational Church in Whitechapel. It was a successful metropolitan church with a membership approaching 1,000. In 1832 there was a revival at Wycliffe. Reed was worried by it. 'I invited the servants of the families of our congregation, and also the children of pious education, to meet me in the vestry.'[23] He studied accounts of transatlantic revivals (like many prominent Dissenting ministers he maintained increasingly strong links with America) and he read Colton's book.

Reed's conclusions were judicious. He deprecated a slavish imitation of American ways, he admitted that 'a good deal of what is done in America might be done in Wales, but not generally in England',

and he wrote from his heart, 'A great responsibility is on me. I alike fear doing too much and doing too little. I am unwilling to speak of this work, lest I feed vanity; and to be silent, lest I decline a means of awakening others. If it is the Lord's work, it will speak for itself.'[24] Perhaps it did, because in successive years in the 1830s Wycliffe Chapel was the scene of revivals. But what is significant is that Reed carefully promoted them. He was a fastidious and precise man, a tireless organizer who was respected in the grander world. Something of this organization was reflected in his dealings with revival at Wycliffe. Revival in the 1830s was respectable and very practical as well as being exciting, as befitted 'the arithmetic of faith in God's arrangements'.

It was in this context that Finney became known in England. The revival movement in England in the 1830s and 1840s cannot be compared with that in America as the circumstances differed in too many respects. But in two ways Finney's impact is of great significance for George Williams and his movement. First, he directed his efforts to small, praying groups, whether in churches or in mutual improvement societies. It was an intense and personal approach which fitted in well with the traditions and atmosphere of English Dissent. This approach, whatever its appropriateness to the rapidly changing conditions of nineteenth-century England,[25] lay at the heart of the early Y.M.C.A. Secondly, as was inevitable with revivalists for whom the emphasis is on experience rather than doctrine, Finney blurred the edges of his theology. His development of Perfectionism caused his rupture with Presbyterianism. He was only a Calvinist of sorts and later the young Spurgeon considered him to be a rank Arminian, but all this was disguised by the intensity of his message. He had himself experienced sudden conversion and his preaching hammered home the sacred duty, and ability, of the individual to repent. Finney lived at an almost impossible spiritual level. Presentable and accomplished in his unregenerate days, as a converted man he preached a gospel devoid of pastel shades. *He* had been saved, how terrible that others *like him* remained in darkness. He knew of the power of salvation, but he knew too much of the carnal world to believe that any serious man could for one moment permit mere amusement to accompany holiness. Mere amusement was a tragic irrelevance when the lives of Christians were *always* to be at the point of perpetual revival.

Such a summary suggests what would have been acceptable to

Williams and to any personable, converted, and therefore serious shop assistants, whose long hours left no time for delightful frivolity, let alone philosophical doubt. The Y.M.C.A. tried to maintain this impossible standard and in his private life Williams found little difficulty in doing so, even when prosperity tempted him with all the leisure in the world. There was none the less a practicality in Finney's approach which characterized both Williams and the Y.M.C.A. Converted men, aware of the treasure within each unconverted soul and painfully aware of the old Adam within themselves, are well placed to turn this old Adam to good account in others, particularly if the challenge of seeking material wealth has already developed the arts of presentation and persuasion – as all good drapers' assistants knew.

In one other respect Finney's impact is of the greatest importance. Williams held a lasting belief in the efficacy and techniques of revivalism when even his most revered associates, Lord Shaftesbury among them, expressed doubt. In his later years Williams supported campaigns and entertained the campaigners, and time and again they were men spiritually descended from Finney, developing his theology, and seeking to strengthen his influence.

Notes

1. *Time*, 12 June 1944 (Johnson Cuttings).
2. J. E. Hodder Williams, *The Life of Sir George Williams*, 1906, p. 3 *et passim*.
3. H. Begbie, *The Ordinary Man and the Extraordinary Thing* n.d. pp. 9–10.
4. I am grateful to the Somerset County Archivist for this information.
5. Correspondence.
6. I am grateful to the Bridgwater Borough Librarian for this information.
7. Hodder Williams, op. cit., p. 15.
8. Information.
9. *The Times*, 20 January 1906.
10. Hodder Williams, op. cit., p. 27.
11. I am grateful to the Revd. D. H. Cummins for this information.
12. Correspondence.
13. Hodder Williams, op. cit., p. 45. The brother was W. F. Williams, who seems subsequently to have become a grocer and tea dealer.

14. *Diary*, 27 November 1844.
15. Quoted in G. F. Nuttall, *The Significance of Trevecca College 1768–1791*, 1969, p. 8, p. 19.
16. *Annual Report of the Somerset Congregational Union . . . Centenary Number 1896* (Wellington, 1896) p. 52.
17. For Evan James, 1802–69, see *Congregational Year Book*, 1870, p. 307.
18. See for instance W. E. Shipton 'The History of the Young Men's Christian Association of London', *Lectures delivered before the Young Men's Christian Association 1845–46*, 1864, vol. 1, p. xxxviii; *The Examiner*, 16 November 1905 (Selwyn Cuttings); Hodder Williams, op. cit., p. 28 *et seq.*
19. *Morning Leader*, 11 November 1905 (Selwyn Cuttings).
20. Hodder Williams, op. cit., p. 31 *et seq.*
21. See 'C. G. Finney 1792–1875' *Dictionary of American Biography*. 1931, vol. VI, pp. 394–6.
22. John Kent, 'American Revivalism and England in the Nineteenth Century', *Papers Presented to the 'Past and Present' Conference on Popular Religion*, 7 July 1966, p. 9.
23. A. and C. Reed, *Memoirs of . . . Andrew Reed, D.D.*, 1863, p. 154.
24. ibid., pp. 155–6.
25. Kent, art. cit., p. 22 *et seq.*, p. 34.

CHAPTER III

'Let such a man become an evangelical preacher': The Pulpit World of the Metropolitan Dissenter

In the autumn of 1841 George Williams was in London. Henceforward his material prosperity was indistinguishable from that of Hitchcock, Rogers of St. Paul's Churchyard, the business house to which he was now attached. For a decade (it is impossible to be more precise) his spiritual prosperity was associated with that of the most remarkable of all London's Dissenting churches – the King's Weigh House Congregational Church, at that time meeting in Fish Street Hill.

The Weigh House rejoiced in its seventeenth-century ancestry. Its recently erected buildings were costly for their time, its congregation was large and opulent, and the fellowship exercised its duties regularly and seriously. Even the world of a metropolitan chapel was still circumscribed, but to ambitious countrymen the Weigh House was a gateway to every prospect. Within inevitable limits, the church had great business standing, some social standing, and increasing political standing. Within its fellowship met all the strands of England's interconnected and self-sufficient Dissenting underworld. George Williams (number 422 on the roll and the second George Williams to be in membership), exercised the privileges of membership from December 1842.[1] For some years he was regular in attending the ordinance and such was the nature of the Weigh House and the Nonconformist world that he could never be far from its associations.

Among those already in membership were G. W. Conder, a student at Highbury College who during his ministry in Leeds would support the Leeds Y.M.C.A., and a youth from Rotherham, Samuel Habershon, who in later years as a fashionable physician would be prominent in the London Y.M.C.A. Habershon illustrates the complexity of the Dissenting world. During the 1840s he lodged at Billiter Square, the home of his kinsman Ebenezer Smith and Smith, likewise a physician, was the son of John Pye Smith, the most attractive and learned of Congregational divines. In 1846 Ebenezer Smith became treasurer of the Weigh House Domestic Mission with which he maintained a lifelong concern and with which George Williams became closely associated. It was easy to be drawn into the criss-crossing world of societies, philanthropies and cousins. Samuel Morley, a lifelong benefactor of the Y.M.C.A., already a rich man and later reputed to be the richest commoner in England, and second to none in his largesse, had been in membership since 1836. In January 1844 Edward Valantine,* one of Williams's fellow assistants and a founder of the Y.M.C.A., became a member and in December 1845 a Windsor lad, still in his teens and habitually attired in blue coat and brass buttons and who was to be intimately connected with both the Y.M.C.A. and the Williams family, was proposed and accepted, taking his first communion the following January. He was Matthew Henry Hodder, assistant to Mr Wilkins, publisher, of Postern Row.†

But remarkable as the fellowship was, the pastor was more so. Thomas Binney was in his early forties. In 1829 he had succeeded John Clayton, a gentlemanly person whose manners vied with his Conservatism, and for forty years he sustained a totally different sort of ministry, varying in intensity over the years but never in faithfulness. There were combined in Binney all the excellencies and the faults of the Nonconformist minister. He was both divinely inspired and highly professional. On all possible counts save that of temperament he was an ideal subject for young men's hero worship.

Binney was striking in appearance. In his earlier years there was a frailty about him which his admirers found indescribably appealing. The Weigh House deacon who first noticed his gifts found him 'tall, thin, eloquent, natural, with a feeble voice and very rapid.'[2] Eleven years later the feebleness of voice had been utilized to produce an intimate, penetrating style of preaching. The frailty in physique now suggested hidden powers: 'He is very tall and athletic, without the

* He appears in the Church Book as Valentine which is how his name was often spelt in afterlife. At this time, however, he spelt it Valantine.
† Hodder joined at the same time as Mrs. Samuel Morley. His was not the only publishing link with the Weigh House. In September 1837 Daniel Macmillan joined the church and in April 1841 his brother Alexander followed suit. It was, however, a brief connexion. *King's Weigh House Church Book* 1794–1867; *The Times*, 19 October 1911.

slightest approach to corpulency. He possesses, no doubt, a robust constitution. His shoulders are high and rather broad, considering the proportions of his figure otherwise; which proportions are better seen on account of his not wearing a gown in the pulpit. He has a fine, pleasant open countenance, with one of the loftiest, best developed foreheads I have ever seen.'[3] This was the Binney Williams knew. By the time he reached his prime, his brow had become even more memorable. Joshua Harrison, a pastor claiming the friendship equally of Binney, Samuel Morley and George Williams, recalled Binney's 'tall figure, his massive head, his keen eye, his commanding presence, and his marvellous intellectual power'.[4] Paxton Hood succumbed to his 'vast stalwart frame, blue, shrewd, tender eye, and light brown hair',[5] and the frontispiece to a memorial volume portrays a man in appearance somewhere between Oliver Cromwell and H. H. Asquith.[6]

His character matched his appearance. Binney was a complicated man with many shadows, 'his was a broad, restless, active, even irritable intelligence'.[7] He was a little too conscious of his abilities, cultivating eccentricities and at times presuming upon his reputation. He was a tense and often melancholy man, prone to irritability and frequently suffering from mental and physical collapse. He was also a *desultory* man.[8] He was no administrator; preaching came a little too easily. Binney gave the impression of being a man who could turn his hand to most things, yet whose outward ability would never adequately reflect the inward powers. Intellectual admirers felt that the discipline of a university would have transformed his life.[9] It would also have taken him far from the Weigh House.

But this self-conscious, questing, unfulfilled man was also wonderfully perceptive, giving as well as seeking sympathy. This part of him was reflected in his letters, in his smile and in his conversation. For thirty of his years at the Weigh House, Binney was unquestionably a public figure. He was also pre-eminently a *man* in an age which venerated manliness as akin to greatness, and very English. His influence on an attached congregation in which, remarkably, young men outnumbered young women, could only be profound.

The membership of a great London church was peculiarly fluid, unduly depending on the neighbourhood or the preacher's power or the mobility of his auditory. The Weigh House reflected this, but in the decade after 1835 its membership grew from under 250 to nearly 450.[10] The chapel itself held over 1,500 and it was seldom empty,

'. . . as Mr. Binney presents one of the most remarkable heads among the preachers of the metropolis, so his pews show a finer set of heads, more square, intelligent, and nineteenth-centuryish, than any other pews perhaps in the kingdom'.[11] Thus it was in 1851, and so it was at his passing over twenty years later: '. . . there was a prestige in the Weigh House. It had been the Nonconformist Cathedral of Wealth, and of the middle-classes . . . and Thomas Binney was supposed very worthily to represent those imperial Tribunes of the Chambers of Commerce. There was a large detachment from this regiment of the Life Guards of England at Stamford-hill on Monday [for his funeral service] . . . He was Minister to the great peerage of the comfortable side of life. . . .'[12] But this peerage (and of his church members Samuel Morley in fact refused a peerage) was of the first creation. These comfortable men were self-made men, like their minister, and this provided a bond second only to evangelical certainty between pastor and people, aspiring shop assistants among them.

Inevitably, an individualistic age is concerned with personal success and at least one of the secrets of the influence of Nonconformist parsons was that they were eminently successful self-made men. Binney had been invited to his important charge when he was in his early thirties. His education had been snatched when and where he could. He knew precisely what it meant to be a shop assistant – in his case to be a bookseller and printer – and he never entirely lost the imprint of those years. The fanciful traced certain mannerisms in the pulpit to his type-setting days.

Perhaps only his call to the ministry had saved both his spiritual and his secular life, and that alone widened Binney's sphere of usefulness. So it is not strange that his most successful publication, reaching fifteen editions and selling 100 copies daily in its first year (excluding Sundays) should have the suggestive title *Is It Possible to make the best of both Worlds?* (1853).[13] Neither is it surprising that his answer, whatever the many important qualifications, should have been 'yes' and that this seeming gospel of gold should be neither forgotten nor forgiven. Anglicans were particularly critical. Few could agree with J. H. Gurney's appreciation of Binney's 'true philosophy, vivid eloquence and chastened wit'[14] and in an obituary notice *The Guardian* commented: 'No one who can entertain the question and answer it as Dr. Binney did, whether it is possible to make the best of both worlds, can have a large measure of high spiritual power.'[15] Yet how suggestive it was of the climate of Victorian Nonconformity and how suggestive too that the book originated in a lecture to young men or that that lecture should have provoked a controversy amongst subsequent lecturers to the Y.M.C.A. at least until 1860.*

Clearly, Binney was a self-made young man's man, whose appeal was rather more sophisticated than C. G. Finney's. George Williams joined the Weigh House when his life was already promising. It was precisely and purposely to such young men that Binney addressed his appeals:

'. . . he supposes the youths around him to be familiar with the thoughts of the time; he supposes their hearts to be heavy with aspirations peculiar to their age; and he flings his whole soul into his speech to them, and aims to be their captain – their leader; to utter to them the inspiring words, to cheer them to the battle of life. We know no other preacher who so truly preaches to his auditors the reality that life *is* a battle, and who presents the warfare in so hearty and glorious a tone; he never whines sentimentally about the shots that fly over the field; he does not scent his hearers with rose-water philanthropies; he points to the opposing forces, or the ambushed foes – life's temptations and sorrows, and disappointments, and says, "Up, and at them!"'[16]

This was surprising enough. More remarkably, Binney did this humorously and perceptively, 'look at all things – prices and people – how they buy and how they sell – the sellers and the purchasers – the hours of labour and the hours of rest; try to look at all; try to know the whole tariff of trade; . . . You are teachers! . . . Know, then, the world's thoughts and the world's ways, that you may be the world's masters and ministers'.[17] Thus Binney is reputed to have addressed a group of ministerial students whom a previous speaker had urged to eschew worldly vanities. More revealing is his treatment of the dying lad tormented by the fear that there were no books in heaven, 'And, my dear boy, they tell me that you are only sorry to die because you will be able to read no more books . . . but you know you are going amongst the *souls of books*: amongst the souls of the men who thought the books. You will not need clumsy paper and type; you

* E. Paxton Hood, Thomas Binney: *His Mind, Life and Opinions*, 1874, pp. 168–74. The lecture, delivered in the winter of 1851–2, was not one of the official Exeter Hall series of Y.M.C.A. lectures, although several of the Exeter Hall lecturers commented upon it.

will be reading the very essence of things. . . .'[18] The story – alas only anecdotes survive to depict Binney's influence – sheds a subtle light upon the Victorian preoccupation with death. It was thus that he sought to interpret the verities of Evangelical religion to his young men, George Williams, Matthew Hodder, Edward Valantine, Samuel Morley and Habershon among them.

It was also in this way that Binney held the allegiance of many who had achieved prosperity. If he emphasized his mission to the young he also emphasized his mission to the middle classes, and in the complicated England of that time shop assistants were on the further fringes of those classes, a fact which the Y.M.C.A. later stressed. It was Binney who told the Congregational Union in his chairman's address of May 1848: 'Our special mission is neither to the very rich nor to the very poor. We have a work to do upon the thinking, active, influential classes – classes which fill neither courts nor cottages, but which, gathered into cities, and consisting of several gradations there, are the modern movers and moulders of the world.'[19]

Such sentiments have long ceased to be fashionable or even admirable, but they were dynamic. Binney's assertion, like many notorious statements, was torn from its context. He was speaking in the midst of the Year of Revolutions, and the prospect excited him: 'Revolutions are convulsing the world, and they are doing so partly through the medium of ideas consecrated by us . . . and, it must be confessed, that if our ideas be right, or, whether right or wrong, if they should predominate, our mission is, and would seem to be, revolutionary.'[20] If the middle classes were indeed the thoughtful class in so stirring an age, then how magnificent to devote one's life to stimulating their thoughts and how providential to be stimulated by such a man. Binney acted thus to Samuel Morley, fast becoming Nonconformity's most representative and influential layman. He unavailingly urged Morley to become a deacon of the Weigh House in 1846, he baptized Morley's children, he keenly followed Morley's political career, and a relationship developed of admiration on the minister's side and devotion on the millionaire's. Morley was not a subtle man, but a Binney-dominated man could not be of light weight.[21]

A lesser but not dissimilar relationship developed with another millionaire, J. J. Colman of Norwich who, like Morley, became a benefactor to the Y.M.C.A. In the 1850s, members of the widely-spread Colman clan took sittings at the Weigh House.[22] Later the young Colmans, like the young Morleys, were baptized by Binney[23] –

a fact worth recording in view of the tightly knit Dissenting world and of the deference afforded to philanthropic wealth by the organizers of philanthropy. It really did seem that such men moved and moulded the world.

It remains to consider the nature of Binney's appeal. It was of course cemented by his compelling pulpit power. Yet he was a most uneven preacher and his style varied over the years. In 1857, Binney returned from a prolonged visit to Australia, a mellower man. He usually eschewed notes and the more obvious tricks of eloquence. He would seem to shuffle his way through an argument at first uncertainly, 'running his hand through his hair, hastily, throwing out his long right arm, the thumb closed upon the two fore-fingers', gradually feeling that he was catching what he sought until 'the left hand brought forward, and the fingers of the other hand resting upon it – sentence after sentence cleared out into the light, and revealed that he had now made his way. Then the start back, the glance round to the gallery, usually to the right; and the close of that portion of the discourse reached, a deep sigh, sent forth from the chest . . .'[24] Then would come humour and an intimacy of approach which was disconcerting because there was little familiarity in the worshipful atmosphere of the Weigh House. 'Throughout his preaching . . . he used very little colour, but his words, especially by the effect of his *accent* of voice and *hand*, had . . . all the effects of colour . . . I believe he was the greatest master of *accent* in speech in our day. . . . He had a singular power of *whispering* in the pulpit, but the whisper made itself heard over the whole average audience. It was passion informing accent, and producing . . . colour', and Paxton Hood, thus describing his hero, comments that it is here, where only accent may enter the soul, that oratory is closest to song.[25]

A good preacher is all things to all men. Binney could startle, as if to remind men that sympathy is only possible in a cruel world, 'It would be a terrible world, I do think, if it was not embellished by little children; but – it would be a far more terrible one if little children did not die.'[26] He could appeal to the unsophisticated: 'Upon my word, I saw the creature; I heard the bones rattle and the teeth chatter!' was the memory of one who heard him on the text 'There is a skeleton in every house'.[27] But Binney's main pride was in the careful development of an argument whose stages his auditors missed at their peril. He paid his hearers the compliment of believing that their intelligence was more developed than it was and, because his was a self-confident congregation, the results were gratifying. 'We were nothing, and deserved nothing, and He made us *men* – placed us here, with our foot on the earth and our face to the sky – the lords of the world, with heads for thought and hands for action . . . Why, to be a *man*, simply A MAN, and nothing more, is so much . . .' It was stimulating to hear this from one whose evangelical orthodoxy was seldom in doubt. How much more so that this was said in the course of a funeral sermon.*

It may be true that Binney 'lowered the style of preaching from the oratorical to the conversational and raised the standard of worship from the extemporary to the liturgical'.[28] Binney's preaching, though demanding, need in itself have little lasting effect. He was not prone to measure his success by the number of souls brought to decision in the course of a sermon. But Binney's church was as truly gathered a fellowship as a city cause embracing millionaires and apprentices within its membership could be, and its services were not merely vehicles for pulpit pyrotechnics. The normal, successful chapel tended to breed an atmosphere of fracas. Pew sittings were let (at the Weigh House only 200 were free) and it was only when the service had begun and the subscribers were ensconced that the poor or the country visitors or the sermon-tasters could be seated. There was always an irritating rush and rustle. Binney was a pioneer in the reformation of Nonconformist worship.

The atmosphere of the Weigh House was intensely worshipful and the accoutrements of worship were carefully considered. Binney himself was neither very musical nor at all mystical and perhaps for this reason his solid congregations could tolerate his attempt to enhance the atmosphere in which they heard the Gospel. He preached to a people who were increasingly aware of culture and who were yet terrified of Romishness. For these his *Service of Song in the House of the Lord* was a godsend. His hymn, 'Eternal Light' remains among the more durable of Victorian hymns, breathing an intensity and a devotion which are in no way sentimental. Henry Allon, himself a pioneer of Dissenting psalmody and pastor of a London church with important Y.M.C.A. associations, was struck by the power of devotion contained within Binney's prayers. He recalled the now aged Binney praying for a full thirty minutes in a way which took his

---

* Hood, op. cit., p. 103. The sermon, 'Light and Immortality Brought to Light by the Gospel', was in memory of Algernon Wells, one of Congregationalism's first ecclesiastical statesmen.

hearers into the presence of God.[29] This quality was not always found in Nonconformist chapels where extempore prayer could be an embarrassing experience. Binney in prayer was 'a devotional man talking intellectually'.[30]

Intellectual yet comprehensible, Binney's theology was acceptable to his people. Once it had seemed adventurous. 'All that I have to say is, that those of you who *want* to have everlasting punishment, may have everlasting punishment!' was supposedly his farewell to his flock at Newport, Isle of Wight.[31] In retrospect, Paxton Hood considered that his Weigh House sermons foreshadowed the deeper thoughts of F. D. Maurice or F. W. Robertson.[32] Yet it was the general feeling that Binney tended to the conservative side of evangelical theology. If his preaching made full use of contemporary applications, it was also eminently scriptural. He regularly preached against the insidious advance of rationalism disguised as German criticism. In his belief that creation and salvation 'both rolled on the wheels of law' and there was a 'fore-ordaining and determining' law-giver, he was Calvinistic.[33] Yet Binney intuitively rejected eternal damnation and 'the hard and terrible conclusions of Calvinistic predestination' and then refused to go further. 'He could stand and adore . . . but he would not explore. It was holy ground, and he simply put his shoes off his feet and bowed his head'[34] and hoped for the best.

And such a position was more than adequate for Binney's congregation. In a time of perplexity it was good for men too busy for perplexity of this sort to be told 'it is better that we should not be living under the reign of miracle . . . If it were so, we should never learn the lessons of manhood, never learn the lessons of self-government and self-direction; never be raised up into men able to regulate ourselves . . .'[35] In the end it all came back to earnest manliness.

In May 1853 Lord Shaftesbury, whose connexion with the Y.M.C.A. and with metropolitan concerns generally was still in its early stages, gave a rather brave dinner-party in honour of Harriet Beecher Stowe. It was brave because its guests were varied. 'I rejoice, as a peacemaker, to have brought together the Archbishop of Canterbury and the Rev. Thomas Binney, a flaming Dissenter.'[36] Binney's reputation as a 'flaming Dissenter' was waning by 1853 and in an age of increasingly *political* religious controversy his attitude, like his preaching and his theology, seemed to be almost conservatively moderate. There developed a mutual respect, approaching friendship, between Binney and Shaftesbury. None the less Binney's Dissent was a very conscious thing, and it must be examined for none of his flock could be unaware of it.

Binney's reputation had flamed since 1833 when a sentence in an appendix to the published version of his address at the Weigh House's stone-laying ceremony was snatched out of context. Read in context it was reasonable, if striking. Torn out of context at a time of trouble for the Church of England, it was dreadful: 'It is with me, I confess, a matter of deep, serious, religious conviction, that the Established Church is a great national evil; that it is an obstacle to the progress of truth and godliness in the land; that it destroys more souls than it saves; and that, therefore, its end is most devoutly to be wished by every lover of God and man'.[37]

It was decades before the 'Weigh House Corrosive Sublimate' could be forgiven for this. In fact it does not appear that Binney opposed the *principle* of Establishment – it was its British practice to which he objected. Neither does he appear to have had profound objections to episcopacy, indeed he would have made a not inadequate prelate himself. He was increasingly conspicuous by his absence on the political platforms of Dissenting England, and if politics ever appeared in his pulpit it was because his hearers were drawing, in manly earnest fashion, their own doubtless logical conclusions. Yet Binney remained a prominent Dissenter and this entailed political bias. He was an effective pamphleteer at a time when the pamphlet was losing its effectiveness, and in Samuel Morley his congregation had one of England's leading Nonconformist Liberals. In November 1868, when Morley was at last on the verge of a not unsuccessful career in the House of Commons, Binney wrote to him, 'Hurray! Hoorah!! All right. More than two thousand ahead. Glorious!!! We have had three telegrams, each more and more encouraging. We waited anxiously for the last. It has just come, and we are so glad. All possible congratulations . . . and now we drink to the member for Bristol. . . .'[38]

Perhaps it was enough that Binney made his support clear for the party which represented what was most progressive (and successful) in English life, without condoning the hopes of its wilder Dissenting fringes. He was consistent in his attitude, despite the annoyance of more enthusiastic brethren. But in one respect Binney's influence was signal. English middle-class people, English Liberals, and increasingly English Nonconformists (it is tempting to confuse the three) saw themselves as a civilizing force. Binney shared this sense of mission.

He showed ambitious men that it was possible for Dissent at home and in chapel to be 'raised above all narrowness and vulgarity'.[39] He showed that in worship, 'singing is no more to be performed by instinct or miracle, than any other duty'.[40] He was at times painfully explicit. At an ordination near London, Paxton Hood recalled how Binney interrupted his address with a comment on Christian courtesy, and how he illustrated this with an experience remembered thus:

'He was preaching, he said, in a chapel, not overcrowded, and in one of the aisles of the chapel stood a young woman, apparently not too strong or robust, leaning on a pew in which were two young men – only two young men – and "would you believe it?" said the preacher, "there they sat, and never opened the pew door for the young woman; and there was no occasion for them to vacate their seats, although that might not have been too much in a crowded chapel – had they been gentlemen, and had she been a servant girl. No! there she stood, and *there* they sat! How strange the coincidence", continued the preacher; "it was just such a chapel as this; the aisle was just like yonder aisle; ay! it was just this day of the week too, just this day of the month – yes, and this very year, *and – and* in this very place; it is this very night; *there* the aisle! *there* the pew!"'[41]

Surely only a most enveloping personality could take such liberties with young men, even in the greatest days of the pulpit. That this was done (and similar tales are told of other and later preachers) suggests the preacher's long-vanished power. It was this power which moulded George Williams until he was ready to mould and to move others.

The threads of Binney's influence must be drawn together. He possessed one great advantage – he shared the limitations of his flock. He too was self-made and his homes, first in Kennington and South-wark, then in Camden Town and finally at Doric Lodge, Upper Clapton, were precisely their sort of residence. He too strained after a higher life, without succumbing to fancies and affectations. What his obituaries noticed as a weakness was in fact his strength. *The Spectator* seized on this, 'His were the qualities of a strong, limited, sagacious, earnest, not specially refined, and by no means mystic, religious nature . . .', his feeling for art 'was keen and sound so far as it went', he was in short 'a safe model and a sound teacher – if not of the highest kind – for thousands of men, and the kind of men who make our English state so solid and trustworthy as it is'.[42] *The Spectator* cannot have known 'Eternal Light', otherwise its assessment stands. No other man could so have influenced the Weigh House congregation at that time, and the impression must remain of a man who was one of the main, if not *the* main, moulders of the spirit of the Y.M.C.A.

Of the five Weigh House men who were members in the 1840s and were prominent in the Y.M.C.A. – Habershon, Valantine, Hodder, Williams, and Morley – only Samuel Morley died still in membership. By 1856 the others had withdrawn from the Weigh House, though their interest in some of its activities remained. They were ceasing to be impressionable young men and their homes were already in the suburbs. Binney was passing his prime and he had already influenced them. Inevitably his was a transitional influence and perhaps his preaching was too much of a *disintegrating* power. Some of his young men, like Daniel and Alexander Macmillan, moved on to the more enticing pastures of Broad Church Anglicanism. Others, like Williams, returned to a safer Evangelicalism, also within the state church. Some, like Matthew Hodder, did so within another Nonconformist Church. But Williams never ceased to be affected by the influence of Binney. His diary for the 1840s says little that is revealing of Binney and it is in Valantine's diary that uncritical devotion shines. What is revealing is that in the course of the frequent debates in the Y.M.C.A. as to the true place and nature of educational and recreational agencies within the movement, Williams never openly sided against them. He distrusted them, but just as unconverted men could not become *members* of a Congregational Church or of a Y.M.C.A., and just as many good members appreciated such agencies, so Williams could not in Christian humility question the sincerity of fellow converts once admitted to the fold. What might seem to be a mark of the exclusiveness of a Nonconformist church or of a Y.M.C.A., was in fact a guarantee of wisdom and tolerance. The members were spiritual brothers.

In this, Williams was more Binney's heir than Finney's, and if he retained his belief in Revivalism he also developed a remarkable power of prayer. When the preaching and the controversy had died away, it was the atmosphere of devotion surrounding his conduct of worship which men most remembered about Thomas Binney. 'Withal he was very manly.'[43]

In the tight world of London Dissent where the pulpit was the only theatre tolerable for the pious, Binney's could not be the sole influence on George Williams. In fact he sat under many preachers, but there was one of particular importance for him in the early 1840s. He was John Leifchild of Craven Chapel, a man more typical of the London pulpit than Binney. An account of him reveals the connexions complicating Williams's world.

Among Williams's early London acquaintances was Mr. Cutting of New Oxford Street. Cutting was a most religious man, offering open house to students at the London theological colleges, promoting open-air preaching at vantage points in the metropolis and delving into the alleyways of Paddington and Westminster as well as Mayfair and Soho. The Cuttings offered a second home for Williams and an opportunity for wide usefulness, and through Cutting, Williams sometimes attended Craven Chapel. The links multiply. Leifchild was an early supporter of the London City Mission, with which Williams came into increasing contact. One of Leifchild's deacons was a governor of the workhouse in Dean Street close to some of the capital's most notorious streets, and therefore a stamping ground for Cutting and his protégé. Leifchild felt a particular concern for 'that interesting class, the young of both sexes . . .' on whom he looked with 'indescribable solicitude'.[44]

Above all, Leifchild's ministerial career demonstrated the interlocking of the Nonconformist world. He regarded John Clayton, Binney's predecessor at the Weigh House, as his spiritual father. Leifchild's first charge was very nearly at the Surrey Chapel which has an honoured place in Y.M.C.A. pre-history, but was in fact at the Kensington Chapel whose subsequent pastors were all firm supporters of the Y.M.C.A. The first list of Vice-Presidents of the Y.M.C.A. included Binney of the Weigh House, Sherman of the Surrey Chapel, Stoughton of the Kensington Chapel, and Leifchild of Craven Chapel.[45] Mr. Cutting was among the subscribers. A final link concerns the Hitchcock family, Williams's future kinsmen by marriage. The Leifchilds and the Hitchcocks were on friendly terms. The Leifchilds visited the establishment at St. Paul's Churchyard, and Charlotte Hitchcock, one of George Hitchcock's sisters, was married by Leifchild at the Craven Chapel.[46]

These links culminate with the farewells held in Leifchild's honour on 2 May 1854. They involved a public meeting which lasted from 11 in the morning to 3.30 in the afternoon and a public dinner at the Freemasons' Hall in the evening. At the former, George Wilson, deacon, friend and workhouse governor, expatiated on his pastor's career: 'Christ and His Cross has been all his theme. . . . Christ has been exalted; Christ has been extolled; Christ has been set high' in every sermon. And he drew attention to Leifchild's Christian Instruction Society, the body in which Cutting and his friends participated, involving 100 church members in house to house visitation each Sunday, meeting in this way about a thousand families and then maintaining a paid missionary to follow up their Sabbath labours. At the dinner the speakers included Thomas Binney and 'a well-known layman', George Hitchcock. Hitchcock spoke as an Episcopalian and he protested too much. None the less he acclaimed Leifchild as 'a child of God – one with whom they may hope to spend eternity' and in the course of his terse, pointed, and manly speech, he revealed that Leifchild like himself and indeed like George Williams, belonged to that class of professors who never fail to speak a word in season. 'Our dear friend is the only minister who ever spoke to me in an omnibus about my soul. It shows what the man was about . . . and I honoured and loved him for it'.[47]

Thomas Binney was unique; John Leifchild was in the run of Victorian pulpiteers. Like Binney he was a self-made man from the edges of respectability, largely self-educated. Both had experienced the 'drudgery of trade', Binney for a bookseller, Leifchild in a brewery. Both had risen from this drudgery in the only possible way – through the Dissenting ministry. Binney had been born a Presbyterian, Leifchild a Wesleyan Methodist and both gravitated to moderate Calvinism. They were both handsome men. Leifchild, who was in his sixties when George Williams encountered him, was a large, square-headed gentleman with a spade for a jaw and shrewd, rather humorous eyes.[48] His disposition was sunnier than Binney's. It was almost insouciant, at least where money was concerned. If Leifchild's personality was far less compelling, it was yet characterized by a natural charm. He was a family man and his family circle was cultured, embracing sculptors and men of letters as well as parsons and estate agents all attendant on his ministry. His son John was a professional writer, his nephew Henry was a prolific sculptor in the Victorian manner, another nephew, James Baldwin Brown, became one of Congregationalism's most attractive leaders. Their names figure occasionally in Y.M.C.A. reports.*

* Thus Kennington Y.M.C.A. first met in Baldwin Brown's Claylands Chapel. *Fifth Annual Report*, 1849–50, p. 29.

This is stressed lest it be too easily assumed that Leifchild was a shallow man. He was himself a writer of popular devotional works and three increasingly successful pastorates at Kensington, at Bristol, and from 1831 at the Craven Chapel, had provided ample opportunity for published sermons. They had also made disciplined study impossible.

In the course of a prolonged and successful pastorate a church comes to resemble its minister, and vice versa. The Craven Chapel, Foubert's Place, Oxford Street, was different from the Weigh House. It was without traditions. It had been built in the early 1820s as a pious speculation by Thomas Wilson, one of Congregationalism's most active laymen. Wilson loaned £12,000 for the purpose and the result, holding 2,000 people, was 'plain, square, and vastly capacious, with its four deeply-pewed galleries, and with its iron gallery again all round over these'.[49] The situation was promising. Rather obscurely placed in the warren of streets later made fashionable by Carnaby Street, it was yet very close to New Oxford Street and the respectable districts north of that thoroughfare.

Everything depended on the power of a minister to attract a congregation. There was no existing Church fellowship, and only a popular preacher could hope to attract regular pew rents and thus pay off the chapel debt. Leifchild succeeded. He was the first full pastor, and the debt was paid by 1846[50] and he gathered a full congregation of 'thriving merchants and mechanics'.[51] At his height as a preacher the membership was 900 and the chapel was usually filled, and in 1854 when Leifchild retired the membership was still 500.[52] It included some notable people like the scientist Edwin Lankester who had been in membership since 1834 and was the first layman to be asked to give one of the Y.M.C.A.'s Exeter Hall lectures.* The powerful Baines family of Leeds worshipped there when in London.[53] It was in fact a very *family* membership. At the Weigh House the rows of young men attracted comment. At Craven Chapel it was the family pews. The services lacked the devotion of the Weigh House, although the full singing associated with congregations of 2,000 was a feature of them, and the chapel societies were legion. Leifchild himself started fourteen.[54] Although materially Craven Chapel was more successful than the Weigh House, it lacked the

* The lecture, on the Natural History of Creation, was given in 1847. Lankester had transferred his membership from the Congregational church in Saffron Walden to Craven.

latter's timelessness. More obviously the product of its age and its pastor, it barely outlived them. It was too much of a preaching house.

But then Leifchild was in his way a remarkable preacher. If he was unwilling to stick firmly to Calvin or to any creed, there was yet nothing unorthodox in his content; if his message was at times terrible and always emotional, this was expected and cherished by his congregation. Perhaps it was more tolerable for Williams than a diet solely of Binney. Leifchild was of the class of preacher whose sermons 'moved like a procession, and came to an end like a tragedy'.[55] In his younger days he had been gently admonished by one of the great rough old spellbinders: 'your smooth sentences run off the mind as water off marble'.[56] 'From the first', Leifchild admitted, 'I determined to be a *good preacher*, and I have never seriously aimed at anything else all my life', and his nephew recalled, 'He was essentially the preacher, the preacher's word was the joy, the preacher's power was the glory of his manhood'.[57] This was a yearning common to many leading ministers of the time. Andrew Reed expressed the same desire when he wrote, 'I have never yet preached as I desire. It is my *passion* . . . A man must *almost* die, however, to conceive and to preach in the first style of eloquence'.[58] Leifchild reached this first style. T. N. Talfourd, the ex-Dissenter who became a fashionable playwright and lawyer, noted of his Kensington days, 'His manner of level speaking is slovenly . . . but when he is aroused he pours forth a torrent of voice and energy.'[59] Talfourd was particularly impressed with the preacher's description of damnation and this impression was shared by most.

Leifchild was careful of his effect. He addressed his flock without notes, beginning in the lowest of tones to compel attention. 'Begin low, Proceed slow, Take fire, Rise higher; Be self-possessed, when most impress'd'.[60] His rapport with his congregation was complete. He drew them with a power considered to be pure electricity by more than one sermon-taster, 'we were kept spellbound by the hour together'.[61] Like all great preachers, Leifchild possessed the art of arousing a communal emotion while yet speaking to each one of his hearers:

'There was no escape for you in generalities. Down there indeed, in the midst of the densely-seated multitude, no one knew or heeded you; or yonder up there, in the seven-pewed galleries, you were but one in a mountain of heads. But as you looked up to the pulpit, and listened ... you felt yourself individualized ... the terrors of hell get hold upon you. A tremendous doom hangs sword-like over you. The fearful secrets of retributive wrath are now about to be disclosed to you. Smoke ascends from the bottomless pit; doleful wailings assail your affrighted ears. ...'[62]

It was no wonder that 'the congregation sat as paralysed till men held their breath, and women sobbed in the intensity of their excitement'.[63] Baldwin Brown noted this with approval, although he was never himself that sort of preacher. But then, for him, it all came back in the end to manliness: 'where was the power? It was himself! It was the man, the very soul of manliness, the very soul of godliness projected into his ministry'.[64]

Even the most successful preachers learn of their effect in devious ways. Leifchild's son and biographer tells a terrifying story which sets his father in context. Visiting Chatsworth, his father was shown the pleasure grounds by an under-gardener who, he learned, had once attended Craven Chapel but had since lapsed:

'"Who preached there?" I enquired. "An old gentleman", said he, "and it was a large congregation". "Did his ministry make no impression on you?" continued I. "Yes it did, and often frightened me all the Sunday nights; but it went away again on the Monday mornings". "Young man", said I, looking him solemnly in the face, "I shall be a witness against you at the Judgment Day." "Against me, Sir!" rejoined he, starting back; "against me, Sir! for what?" "Because," I continued, "I have called upon you to embrace the Gospel, and you have rejected it. I am the minister you heard at Craven Chapel. I must witness against you at the last, as I witness against you now." "Good God," he exclaimed, "who would have thought it?" and he walked away sighing, so that I could get no further information from him.'[65]

This encounter apparently took place in 1845 or 1846. This was George Williams's Leifchild. In 1844 shortly before the Y.M.C.A. was formed, Williams and Valantine heard him preach a sermon for young men at Craven Chapel. This time the seed was curiously fruitful. If Leifchild was not unaware of the fruit he was ignorant of the seed, for his son thus dismisses 1844: 'No particular event, either personal or ministerial, in the year 1844, called for particular notice;

and of that year, therefore, there is no particular record. Constant work and continued success probably characterized this one, like many others at Craven Chapel. Perhaps the absence of record sufficiently proves that it was one of peace as well as prosperity'.[66]

* * * *

'Given, a man with moderate intellect, a moral standard not higher than the average, some rhetorical affluence and great glibness of speech, what is the career in which, without the aid of birth or money, he may most easily attain power and reputation in English Society?. . . Let such a man become an evangelical preacher . . .'[67]

The diaries of George Williams and his friend Edward Valantine are meticulous in their mention Sabbath by Sabbath of the preachers under whom the young men sat. Thomas Binney and John Leifchild have been considered at some length because they were remarkable men of their kind, dominating the churches whose activities most concerned the maturing Williams. But other parsons figure in the diaries, some frequently. Many of them happened to be Congregationalists. All were prominent in their denomination and all were able men. All would appear regularly in the Annual Reports of the Y.M.C.A., and a significant number of them were new to a London pastorate. Their churches were active after the manner of thriving metropolitan chapels, and very often their deacons and elders would be no less concerned with the Y.M.C.A. than their pastors. Their world delighted in coincidences. Again and again there were links between the preachers mentioned in the diaries, the laymen prominent in forming branches of the association, and other movements of the period which could not but feed it.

Dr. Leifchild's connexion with the Y.M.C.A. itself was benign and dignified rather than intimate. He was an ageing man approaching retirement, and it was the pulpit where he was king rather than the meeting with tea and seedcake. Thomas Binney's connexion remained stronger. His name would appear frequently in Reports, he would be among the eminent divines delivering the Exeter Hall lectures,[68] and his church membership continued to include young men, a number of Hitchcocks among them including some of Mr. Hitchcock's nephews. Yet it is a little surprising that Binney's name did not figure more prominently. Perhaps it was because he was entering upon a long autumn. The melancholy and the eccentricity in his character became more pronounced, rather as his power in the pulpit had mellowed. In 1845 he went on a tour of the Americas in search of change. 'How does the poor Weigh House look on a Sunday?' he wrote to Samuel Morley.[69] In 1857, Binney again left England, this time for a triumphal tour of Australia, where the *Sydney Morning Herald* hailed this 'Golden Lecturer to Young England' and it was confidently predicted that the visit was a prelude to retirement in Australia.[70] In fact he did not retire until 1869, and then it was not to Australia, but to Doric Lodge, Upper Clapton. By then the Weigh House was tending to become a memory and Binney had long been the eldest statesman of his denomination.

After Binney, and with Leifchild, the favourite minister was James Sherman of the Surrey Chapel which was the chapel of another of Hitchcock's young men, Edward Beaumont. The Surrey Chapel was a child of the greatest days of the Evangelical Revival. For fifty years it had been the London preaching house of that well-born but earthy great-heart, Rowland Hill. It had been cherished by Selina, Countess of Huntingdon, and it had accumulated a tradition of philanthropies and activities. The Surrey Chapel was a many-sided building so that the Devil might hide in no corner of it, and it held upwards of 2,000. For many years, during the May meetings, it was the scene of the preacher's proudest challenge, the annual London Missionary Society Sermon. It claimed to have housed London's first Sunday School, the Religious Tract Society's first meeting, and that of the Ragged School Union.[71]

It was this side of the chapel's life which attracted both Williams and Valantine. Regularly they attended teachers' meetings held in the chapel and on one such occasion Williams noted wonderingly and, as it happened accurately, 'Abt. 500 employed in educating the poor in connection with this Church 12 school and nearly 4000 children.'[72] Beaumont was no less attracted. From January 1845 to December 1847, first as a probationer and then as a full teacher, he taught at the Chapel's Sunday School.*

As a worshipping community, the Surrey Chapel was equally remarkable. Between the years 1833 to 1846 its membership trebled. There were 500 members in 1833 and 1,463 thirteen years later.[73]

---

* He was proposed on 20 January 1845. He regularly attended teachers' meetings as a probationer and was admitted as a full teacher on 16 June 1845. He resigned on 6 December 1847, and was thanked for his services. Southwark Sunday School Society, *Minute Book 1845–1868*.

Thereafter the membership was seldom less than 900. Its appeal was to many beyond the Congregational body. It was aggressively Protestant, abiding by the Thirty-Nine Articles with the addition of Rowland Hill's characteristic gloss, 'I believe the Pope is Antichrist, and his religion abominable.'[74] At the same time it held tenaciously to a purged form of the Prayer Book liturgy and it took pride in its organ and its chanting. Because the Surrey Chapel was such a preaching centre the usual bustling atmosphere invaded its services. In the 1840s all its sittings were let, those 'not occupied . . . at the reading of the second lesson are appropriated to the use of strangers'.[75] But at times even this could be transformed and on Ordinance Sunday even bustle became inspired. 'One particular feature . . . was the Processional Hymns we always sang in going up to the Lord's Table and in returning to our seats . . . the Administration took from one to one-and-a-half hours and the time was spent in singing hymns . . . Our Morning Service in the grand old days commenced at 10.30, and ended about ten minutes before one. . . .'*

Inevitably, for the Surrey Chapel could hardly be called a fully Congregational church, it was the personality of the ministers which held the place together. James Sherman laboured there from 1836 to 1854. He was an immensely popular preacher who belonged to the older, mellifluous school of oratory. A very gentlemanly person, he was among the last to wear black silk gloves in the pulpit. His sermons, no less than the activities of his flock, drew Williams, Valantine and Beaumont, but they do not seem to have been very demanding. Williams expressed himself as 'delighted' or commented, 'beautiful sermon'.[76] Valantine was no less impressed by the 'dear man in the Lord' and thoughtfully jotted down notes of a sermon on Predestination which might suggest that the 'dear man in the Lord' comfortingly swathed such matters in cotton wool.[77]

There is one further aspect in which Sherman and his chapel are of the utmost interest. It worried many Dissenters that their Sunday Schools for all their apparent success were yet so often separate from their chapels. Few scholars became members. The Surrey Sunday Schools were more intimately linked with their chapel.

In 1846 it was noted that of 136 new members, 85 were under 30 years old, and 59 (the largest group) were between the ages of 20 and

* This was not normal Congregational practice. Congregationalists usually received the elements in their pews. J. W. Read (ed.) *The Christ Church Souvenir Jubilee Book*, 1926, p. 8.

30.* A contributing factor was a well established Young Men's Society. Edward Beaumont remembered that in 1844 the Surrey Chapel already possessed a Young Men's Christian Association, called by that name although 'its objects were altogether different . . . in as much as they met at early morn for prayer and reading essays on Biblical subjects. . . .'[78] It was rather more, however, than a mutual improvement class of the sort common to many chapels. It had been formed in 1840 (its treasurer a Joshua Williams). By 1847 at least one of the branch chapels, that at Castle Yard, also had a Young Men's Association.

Nothing is known of the Surrey Chapel Y.M.C.A. membership beyond the fact that it 'varies much in its members and general prosperity'.† Rather more is known of its aims. It met on Sunday mornings at 6.45 (Castle Yard met on Monday evenings at 8 p.m.). It had been 'established for the purpose of cultivating the talents, and increasing the Scriptural knowledge of its members' and it was the duty of each member to give an address which had previously been vetted by the President. (Castle Yard changed direction in the course of 1847 and now united 'with the pursuit of scriptural knowledge the study of literary subjects'.) The Surrey Chapel Y.M.C.A. had an Annual General Meeting in September and an annual breakfast on Christmas morning. It was carefully supervised by the pastor and church elders who received quarterly reports from it. 'It has been found very beneficial in the training of young men to labours of Christian usefulness.'‡

The association was a long-lived if fluctuating one. In the mid-1850s the Surrey Chapel Y.M.C.A. had become a Sunday prayer meeting run exclusively for young men, in 1860 it was transformed into an association for 'the intellectual, moral, and religious improvement of Young Men', meeting on Thursday evenings in the chapel library each spring and autumn. There was a sessional charge of 1s. 6d. and a diet of lectures, discussions and papers.[79] Perhaps after

* *Surrey Chapel; Its Services and Institutions: with Reports for the Year Ending September 1847*, 1847, pp. 23–4. It is interesting that of the church's 441 occasional communicants, 79 (the second largest group) were Anglican. The new members included a 'Polish nobleman' and three 'of the descendants of Abraham'.

† *Surrey Chapel Report*, 1847, op. cit., pp. 26, 36, 39. The average attendance at Castle Yard was thirty-six.

‡ *Surrey Chapel Report*, 1848, p. 46. By now the Castle Yard Society called itself a Young Men's Mutual Improvement Association, ibid., pp. 49–50.

all it was a Mutual Improvement Society which differed from most only in its elaborate organization. But it bears the distinctive marks of one of David Nasmith's societies.* James Sherman certainly knew of Nasmith and his work for Young Men and City Missions. In 1842, two years after the Young Men's Association was founded, a City Mission Auxiliary was formed at the Surrey Chapel, and in June 1844 the Sunday School ordered for its library John Campbell's newly published and rather flatulent *Memoirs of David Nasmith*. The evidence remains circumstantial,[80] but it is the most direct evidence available that George Williams or some of his friends knew something of Nasmith.

Certainly most friendly relations developed between Hitchcock's Young Men and the Surrey Chapel's Young Men and on Christmas Day 1844, George Williams and seven friends (six of them founder members) went to the annual breakfast. Williams and a Wesleyan friend, J. C. Symons, spoke and Sherman himself took the chair, offering his services and generally speaking 'very delightfully on behalf of the Association connected with the Chapel and also the Young Men's Christian Association meeting at Radley's and thought if both were to meet it would be the means of doing a great deal of good'.[81] The breakfast was the prelude to a fruitful and convivial day. Fruitful because the joint meeting proposed by Sherman did in fact take place,[82] and convivial because back in St. Paul's Churchyard, 'after dinner sat with the worldlings at the wine table in order that no disturbances might arise'. None did arise and that evening, 'the Church that was in the House' took tea together in Symons' bedroom, each converted man being given a number of unconverted brothers for whom to pray.[83] This was the first specific mention of a *system* of prayer of the sort so important to Williams and the founders of the Y.M.C.A.

Sherman's interest in the Y.M.C.A. continued into his semi-retirement to Blackheath in the 1850s. Newman Hall, his very different successor at the Surrey Chapel, carried the connexion between the chapel and the association with him to the triumphantly be-spired Christ Church, Westminster Bridge Road, which replaced the old cause in 1876. For a while the round, devil-less, buildings remained, taken over by the Primitive Methodists who valiantly maintained there an aggressive mission to the lowest orders and then when commercial considerations forced the total abandonment of

* See below, Chapter VII.

Surrey Chapel, the mission was continued elsewhere in the neighbourhood until a new building could be erected. This was opened at great
cost in 1888, on a site only forty yards away. That it was opened at
all was the work of its minister, Benjamin Senior, and a group of
wealthy laymen drawn from all denominations. George Williams
was amongst the most generous of these, and on the thirteenth
anniversary of Senior's ministry, Williams was a guest of honour at
the celebration. He delivered a speech which was immensely genial,
very rambling, and exactly apt for the occasion.[84] Meanwhile, Christ
Church, Westminster Bridge Road, prospered. Lord Kinnaird, whose
father had contributed to its City Mission Auxiliary in the 1840s,
occasionally worshipped there in the 1890s, and also at this time
Joshua Williams, first treasurer of its Young Men's Association in
the 1840s, was a chapel trustee. His fellow trustees included Samuel
Hope Morley whose father, the great Samuel Morley, had laid the
new chapel's memorial stone in 1873, and George Williams whose
life touched upon each of theirs. There is sometimes a charming
symmetry in history.

On 22 October 1843, George Williams worshipped at the Fetter
Lane Chapel. The preacher was the Revd. Caleb Morris, and Williams
professed himself 'much pleased'.[85] The following week Valantine
emulated his friend – he too sat under Mr. Morris. On both occasions
the sermons savoured of the intellectual, and Morris referred particularly to the death of John Foster, the Baptist essayist whom
Leifchild had known well and greatly admired. On the second
occasion Morris spoke too of tolerance, of the Church and the
ministry.[86]

Like the Weigh House, Fetter Lane was proud in its traditions
and of all the metropolitan pulpiteers Morris was closest to Binney
in approach and temperament. He too was melancholic, prone to
nervous prostration and prolonged absence; he too was strangely
uneven in the pulpit and strangely compelling for aspiring young
men. In the last resort he lacked Binney's edge and Fetter Lane
lacked the Weigh House's involved activities, but some felt that at
his height Caleb Morris was without parallel. He was a Welshman
in his early forties and it was the opinion of William Hale White
('Mark Rutherford') who heard him in the 1850s that he outshone
Binney, Gladstone, Cobden, and Bright. 'His eloquence . . . was the
voice of the thing itself.' There was, moreover, a largeness about

Morris: 'He believed undoubtedly in the chief doctrines of Christianity, but he was one of the freest of men, if freedom is the largeness of the space in which we move and live.'[87] Hale White in the 1850s, in his more introverted way, was suffering that London awakening which fell to Williams in the 1840s and his novels contain much that is autobiographical. Hodder Williams suggested that Pastor Bradshaw of Pike Street in *Revolution in Tanner's Lane* was really a portrait of Binney.[88] It is more likely to have been a composite picture owing most to Morris. Both Binney and Morris, like Bradshaw, had a 'singular and contagious power over men',[89] particularly young men, George Williams among them.

> 'The writer of this history remembers when it was his privilege to listen continually to a man whose power over his audience was so great that he could sway them unanimously by a passion which was sufficient for any heroic deed. The noblest resolutions were formed under that burning oratory, and were kept too, for the voice of the dead preacher still vibrates in the ears of those who heard him. And yet, except in their hearts, no trace abides, and when they are dead he will be forgotten, excepting in so far as that which has once lived can never die.'[90]

Morris's connexion with Fetter Lane lasted from 1827 to 1850 when he removed to the West End. Thereafter, Fetter Lane was a declining cause, but its decline contains a brief note of interest. From 1854 to 1855 the pastor was a nephew of George Hitchcock's and a cousin of Williams's by marriage – he was the young Aaron Buzacott.

It was inevitable that with his mission work extending to the alleys of Westminster, George Williams should sample the oratory of Samuel Martin of the Westminster Chapel. Williams heard him in March 1843 and Valantine in June, 'a most beautiful sermon'.[91] Martin became the most popular of mid-Victorian Congregational preachers and the massive, three-tiered Westminster Chapel remains a tribute to his attraction. When Williams first heard him, Martin had been at the chapel for a year. He was a very young man, barely 26, only 4 years older than Williams, and his call to Westminster and the chapel nearest to Buckingham Palace was a sign of unusual promise. Unlike many successful young men he remained fully alive to the needs of young men and his sympathy with the Y.M.C.A. was life-long and had begun in 1845 at the latest. Martin was among the first Vice-Presidents and Exeter Hall lecturers, and his appearance on their platforms was welcomed for the next thirty years.* His death in 1878 evoked a graceful tribute in the normally reticent Annual Reports.[92]

Martin's career no less than Binney's, or Leifchild's, or Sherman's impinges frequently upon this study, emphasizing yet again the inter-connectedness of the world with which we are dealing. Two examples will suffice. In September 1864 as the result of the bicentennial celebrations of the Great Ejectment of 1662 (a commemoration which aroused the concern and on the whole the disapproval of the Y.M.C.A.) Zion Chapel, Bridgwater, was rebuilt on another site. The opening preacher, then at the height of his power, was Samuel Martin.[93] The second link comes from over twenty years previously. Shortly before his arrival at Westminster, Martin was considered for the pastorate of another of the great (and then growing) London chapels – Union Chapel, Islington. The congregation turned him down, eventually preferring another young man of no less promise, Henry Allon.

The present Union Chapel, like the present Westminster Chapel, is a memorial to the power of one man. Allon was more extroverted than Martin. He was perhaps a less accomplished preacher but his was the finer intellect and, as befitted one of Binney's biographers, he was himself musical and a journalist of force and acumen. Allon became his denomination's foremost ecclesiastical statesman, and his connexion with Union Chapel which began in 1844 lasted for nearly fifty years. So did his links with the Y.M.C.A. Two of Allon's deacons, J. W. Willans and Henry Spicer, were in their time no less closely linked. Willans, who was the young Herbert Asquith's uncle and guardian, was on the committee of the London Y.M.C.A. in 1862. Spicer, as befitted one from a large and generous Dissenting family, was associated with Willans in many good causes.[94] It was to the Islington Y.M.C.A. that Edward Valantine later attached himself.

Here again the links mingle in a fascinating confusion. When Allon first preached there the Union Chapel was a pillared edifice, stately for its time. Its origins, like those of the older Surrey Chapel, had been both Evangelical and liturgical. Unlike many chapels it had not been built as a protest at the Establishment, although it

---

* Between 1846 and 1862 he gave eight lectures on a random series of subjects – 'Cardinal Wolsey' in 1848–9; 'Gambling', 1856–7; 'Anglo-Saxon Christianity', 1861–2; and, suitably enough, 'The Instincts of Industry', 1850–1.

could not help being a reproach. In March 1838, six years before Allon's arrival, a Scotsman with a great but disorganized concern for young men transferred his membership from the Maberly Chapel, Hoxton, to Union Chapel, Islington. He was David Nasmith. He first took communion with the fellowship on 4 March, sitting next to Richard Knill, a paragon among early missionaries. The Knills were friends of the Hitchcocks and some ten days previously, on 22 February 1838, Knill had assisted in the ordination of a fellow missionary. He was James Sewell, a Homerton student destined for India. The service was in the Craven Chapel where Dr. Leifchild had only recently married Sewell to George Hitchcock's sister. Offering prayer with Knill was John Williams, so soon to become the martyr of Erromanga. It happened that David Nasmith and John Williams, who both died in the same year, also shared the same biographer – John Campbell. In the 1840s George Williams sat under Campbell and met Knill. Eventually he would be connected with the Sewells by marriage. The one man of whom he does not seem to have known at the time was Nasmith, the work of whose life was also for young men.[95]

A third promising minister was called to the pastorate of a leading London chapel in the early 1840s. He was rather older than Allon and Martin, a cultured and stately man of great learning (or as he preferred to put it, 'extensive information') whose long and distinguished metropolitan career lasted well into the 1880s. From 1843 to 1874 John Stoughton was pastor of the Kensington Chapel. Leifchild had once been minister there and it has never ceased to attract able men both to its pews and its pulpit. Stoughton was the ablest of them all. His chapel was rebuilt for him, in the pillared manner, at the outset of his ministry, and it housed a more socially prominent congregation than was usual for such places.

Stoughton and Allon were cast in the same mould, and as with Allon so Stoughton's connexions with the Y.M.C.A. were almost coterminous with his sojourn in London. He was amongst the first Vice-Presidents and he gave the first of what became the Exeter Hall lectures, on the connexion of Science and Religion.* There are even closer links. For ten years before 1843, Stoughton had ministered at Windsor, and perhaps he was the anonymous man from 'Winsor' who was among the speakers at a May meeting in 1843 which caused

---

* Stoughton's lectures tended to be on historical matters. He was best known as an ecclesiastical historian.

Williams to come away 'convinced of our duty to make more stren-
uous efforts to spread the gospel amongst our own countrymen'.[96]

A year later a local youth, Matthew Henry Hodder, arrived in
London to be apprenticed to a City publisher. Twenty-four years
later in 1868, Hodder went into partnership with John Stoughton's
son T. Wilberforce Stoughton, thus founding the publishing firm
subsequently dominated by members of George Williams's family.

Evangelical preachers regardless of sect were grist to the young
men's mill. Congregationalists were most prominent but perhaps it
was a Baptist whose sermons were most readily appreciated. James
Smith of the New Park Street Chapel in Southwark was an uncut
diamond when compared to any of the Independent pastors.[97] There
was a pithiness about his sermons which particularly appealed to
Edward Valantine who frequently sat under him, learning that Mary
was to be preferred to Martha, that false delicacy was a sin as were
mixed marriages, and on one occasion (this time with Williams)
watching a baptism of six women and a man, 'it was a most affecting
sight'.[98]

The Park Street Chapel epitomized the Dissenting chapel of
literary and sophisticated tradition. It was a seventeenth-century
cause which in its time had attracted distinguished pastors. When
Williams first visited the chapel the buildings were fairly new (it had
been rebuilt in 1833) but they were too close to the river and hemmed
in already by factories and warehouses. It was approached most
easily from the City by way of the Southwark Bridge, which levied a
toll. The attraction of the Blackfriars Bridge, and hence of the Surrey
Chapel, was that it was toll-free.

The congregation, therefore, were particularly dependent on the
power of their pastor, James Smith, 'a quaint and rugged preacher,
but one well-versed in the blessed art of bringing souls to Christ'.[99]
They reflected him in other ways, being a Calvinistic folk with the
'sinews of war'. Their senior deacon, a shortish, stoutish lawyer, was
dapper in a long-tailed coat and old-fashioned silk stockings and
knee breeches, for all the world looking like 'a gigantic robin, chirping
out the verses of the hymn in a piping, twittering voice'.*

It was to the Park Street pulpit, a magnified swallow's nest of a
structure, that a boy-wonder from the fen country first came 'with a

* (C. H. Spurgeon) *C. H. Spurgeon: The Early Years 1834–1859*, 1962, p. 279.
The description is Mrs. Spurgeon's. Her family were long active at New Park
Street.

view' in 1853. To his country eyes it was still a fine enough chapel, 'somewhat in the style of our Cambridge Museum'.* The boy wonder was C. H. Spurgeon who was called to the pastorate in 1854 and so revived the languishing cause, that even when it was rebuilt elsewhere as the Metropolitan Tabernacle, it proved inadequate for its purpose. Spurgeon's pastorate was unique (it could not have been otherwise with a church of 5,000 *members* supporting him) and he had little in common with men like Allon or Stoughton other than a large heart, a Victorian sense of fun and complete sympathy with the Y.M.C.A. Spurgeon became a close friend of Lord Shaftesbury (indeed he was almost the only parson with whom that complicated man felt an easy spiritual affinity) and he was a close associate of Williams helping him with the revived Primitive Methodist version of the Surrey Chapel, and appearing on Y.M.C.A. platforms with great regularity despite the inroads made on his time by his colleagues and his health. It was only proper that Spurgeon lectured to an audience of Young Men on the 'Use of Anecdote' for the Victorian pulpit contained no greater master of that elusive art.†

With another and very different Baptist pastor, we approach Williams's home ground. William Brock's concern with the Y.M.C.A. dated from his arrival in London in 1848. The Bloomsbury Baptist Chapel, of which he was the first pastor, was surely the most eligible Baptist chapel in London. Its style was if anything Romanesque, and with its twin towers and rose window its appearance was undoubtedly handsome. Situated in the heart of Bloomsbury close both to the handsome squares and the appalling rookeries, it could not be other than the spearhead of a forward movement. That it was there at all was due to the largesse of Morton Peto, the most thrusting of Baptist businessmen.

William Brock was already widely known in Baptist circles. As 'Brock of Norwich' and pastor of Norwich's leading Dissenting chapel, the St. Mary's Baptist Chapel, he had the Colmans in his congregation in their Baptist days. As 'Brock of Bloomsbury', he was more widely known. He was not afraid of political involvement and in 1865, when Samuel Morley was embroiled in one of the filthiest of Victorian election fights, Brock wrote to Morley that at

---

* He meant that it had pillars. Even so, was it really 'somewhat' like the glorious Fitzwilliam? See C. H. Spurgeon, op. cit., p. 251.
† *19th Annual Report 1863*, Nat. Council MSS. In 1868 he graced the platform hopping on one foot because of gout. *23rd Annual Report 1867*.

his weekly Communion Service he had prayed specifically for him and his cause 'and all the people responded by an "Amen" that would have sent gladness into your heart'.[100]

Brock was no longer a young man although he remained a young man's man, with his open-air face and his uncomfortable memories of an apprenticeship in Sidmouth. His first public engagement after his removal to London was the delivery in December 1848 of an Exeter Hall lecture on *The Common Origins of the Human Race*. It was an ideal sort of lecture for young men, ranging inquisitively and discursively over the world, airing his knowledge and his prejudices, likening, for instance, the Irish peasants to the 'Natives of Australia' in their appearance and their degradation. Mr. Hitchcock took the chair at his lecture and thereafter Brock's connexion with Hitchcock and his young men was close. Brock's Y.M.C.A. lecture on 'Mercantile Morality' doubtless irritated some employers, but his lecture on the Seventh Commandment was repeated by public request.[101] At the Seventh Annual Meeting (an occasion prompting the comment that 'it is only where Protestantism prevails that there can be gatherings like this', and which was notable for Lord Shaftesbury's presence) the Marylebone Anglican, J. H. Gurney, the Birmingham Wesleyan, G. B. Macdonald, and the Westminster Congregationalist, Samuel Martin, were joined by the Bloomsbury Baptist. Brock's address was a catalogue of self-help, a collection of 'persevering earnestness'. 'All arguments apart, just look at secular life, and ask Mr. Hitchcock and other gentlemen whose names have just been mentioned, if they would give much for a man in their service whose life is not characterized by earnestness . . .'[102]

Earnestness was the worthiest of Victorian virtues – and names – and it was nobly shared by Bloomsbury's Evangelical parsons. Their leader was the Hon. and Revd. Baptist Noel.* Like the rest of them, Noel was a popular preacher commanding the allegiance of a devoted congregation. He was also a public figure in a way that the others were not. He was born in 1798, one of seventeen children, and he belonged to a widely-spreading clan of Evangelical aristocrats. His eldest brother was created Earl of Gainsborough in 1841, and there were connexions by marriage as well as religious sympathy with Lord Ashley himself. From 1827, Noel had been an incumbent of

---

* Baptist Noel, in fact, had a son called Ernest – Ernest Noel, 1831–1931, M.P., Dumfries 1874–85, and long-serving chairman of the Artisans, Labourers and General Dwellings Co.

an Anglican proprietary chapel, St. John's, Bedford Row where in
the heyday of the Clapham Sect, the Thorntons, Wilberforces and
Macaulays had liked to worship. There was another side to the
chapel's history, for St. John's 'at the corner of Chapel-Street and
Great James-Street, was the frequent scene of schism from its first
erection for Dr. Sacheverell: it was subsequently occupied by the
Rev. Mr. Cecil (Low Church); by the Rev. Dr. Dillon, of unenviable
notoriety; the Rev. Daniel Wilson (Bishop of Calcutta); the Rev.
Mr. Sibthorp, given to change; and by the Hon. & Rev. Baptist
Noel, who after 22 years' ministry, preached his farewell sermon here,
Dec. 3, 1848 . . .'*

Noel was the most ardent and vocal of Low-Churchmen. This,
and his felicitous connexions, might explain his position as a chaplain
to the Queen. He was, therefore, doubly welcomed to the platforms
of good causes. He was the Anglican most openly sympathetic to
the founding of the London City Mission, and he was amongst the
earlier London patrons of its originator, David Nasmith. Indeed,
Nasmith's biographer, John Campbell dedicated his book to Noel
who had conferred on the mission the benefit of his 'rank, reputation,
and eloquence'.[103] Noel was a founder of the Evangelical Alliance,
he was keenly concerned in political controversies and did not share
the political conservatism of his family, and he was among the early
supporters of the Drapers' Metropolitan Association and their battle
for shorter hours. Of all Anglicans he was the one most likely to be
admired by Dissenters and he seems to have been the one whose
ministrations were most acceptable to Williams and Valantine, who
sometimes sat under him at St. John's and once heard him deliver a
long speech on shopmen's hours to an overflowing audience at the
Freemasons' Hall.[104]

The question of Evangelical co-operation between Churchmen and
Dissenters was a delicate one even for Noel. In April 1835 he gave
Nasmith some well-chosen advice concerning the proposed London
City Mission. The implications of what he said would no less affect
the Y.M.C.A. ten years later:

'I very much fear, that in the present circumstances of the church,
you will find yourself repelled at every step in *any* plan which

---

* Bishop Wilson was a cousin of Thomas Wilson, builder of Craven Chapel.
J. Timbs, *Curiosities of London*, new ed., 1885, p. 212. For Baptist Noel,
1798–1873, see *D.N.B.*

contemplates the co-operation of different denominations. In the first place, you must secure the consent of the bishop, or you will not get the clergy to act, and without the clergy you will find it hard to move the lay members of the Establishment. In the second place, there is a wide gulf just now between Dissenters and the Establishment. . . . Under these circumstances I know not what course you can take, except to choose between the Dissenters and the Establishment. . . .'[105]

In the 1840s the wide gulf threatened to become unbridgable and in 1848, the year of Brock's arrival in Bloomsbury and Binney's chairmanship of the Congregational Union, and at a time of keen theological debate within the State Church as well as political activity outside it, Noel took an astounding step for a man in his position. He publicly left the Church of England. The issue was the hoary one of Baptismal Regeneration. He was well-advanced into middle-age and although his usefulness could hardly yet be over, his future was uncertain.

Gradually the uncertainty eased. On 25 March 1849, Noel preached in the Regent Square Presbyterian Church. It was the first time he had occupied a Dissenting pulpit. In May he preached for Binney with whom in 1831 he had engaged in a satisfying pamphlet fight which had allowed Binney to write as 'Fiat Justitia'.[106] In August, Noel was publicly baptized in the John Street Baptist Chapel, a stone's throw from his former charge. There for a further twenty years he ministered prominently and acceptably – a second and no less notable Bloomsbury Baptist. He was twice president of the Baptist Union, in 1855 and again in 1867.

Noel's concern for the Y.M.C.A. dated from his Anglican years, and it was as old as that of Sherman, Stoughton, and Samuel Martin. In March 1845, Noel took the chair, as befitted his rank and prominence, at the second of the social meetings held by the association.[107] Among the notables at that meeting was a Presbyterian minister, Dr. Cumming, to whom and to his fellow Presbyterian, James Hamilton, it is necessary to turn, to complete this survey of George Williams's pulpit world.

Both were among the first Vice-Presidents of the Y.M.C.A. and both contributed to the first public lectures, Cumming on Luther, and Hamilton on Christian Botany. Only Cumming figures in the diaries: 'to a Scotch church and heard Dr. Cummin – sermon to the young on the wisdom of Satan – enjoyed it much'; or later, 'very much delighted'. Cumming was also at the meeting on shop hours at which Noel spoke so volubly.[108] It was this perhaps which made him known to Mr. Hitchcock, because in November 1843 he was among the guests at one of the house's functions.[109] Without doubt, Cumming was a most acceptable preacher. Valantine heard him in September 1843, 'and a most delightful sermon we had'. Its gist was that 'illiterate ministers are to be preferred to most eloquent if they preach Christ and his salvation'.[110]

Cumming was not to be ranked with the illiterate, but his reputation was such that Valantine's delight and Williams's enjoyment seem to be explicable only in terms of what C. M. Davies later and unkindly called *gush*. 'Gush is simply the normal condition of those sweetly orthodox folks . . . It is always that dear Earl of Shaftesbury, or dear Poet Tupper and his pension, or dear Dr. Cumming's very last Vial of Wrath, with which they regale you.'[111]

Since 1832, Cumming had been minister of the National Scottish Church at Crown Court, next to Covent Garden. It served as a sort of embassy church for exiled Scotsmen. He rapidly attracted a congregation, pew rents and stipend, which were large even by London standards. In the 1840s, Cumming plunged into controversy, upholding the disrupted Kirk of Scotland in 1843, attacking Rome and the Maynooth Grant in 1845. The Apocalypse was his passion and his belief in the Second Advent and its imminence was a link with Lord Shaftesbury. Cumming had two hobbies – one was apiary, and he wrote frequently to *The Times* signing himself 'Beemaster', and the other was Rome-baiting. In 1844 he published his *Lectures for the Times or an Exposition of Tridentine and Tractarian Popery*.[112]

Cumming was precisely the sort of preacher to irritate the truly intellectual. George Eliot, who never actually heard him, was nonetheless a devastating critic of what he stood for. She condemned the 'Boanerges of Crown Court' for his 'commonplace cleverness' and his tawdry love of ornament, and noted, 'He is essentially a journalist, who writes sermons instead of leading articles.' 'We fancy he is called, in the more refined evangelical circles, an "intellectual preacher"; by the plainer sort of Christians, a "flowery preacher".'[113] There was more than a little truth in this accusation. Cumming's frequent Exeter Hall lectures for the Y.M.C.A. were invariably on subjects which were at once popular and 'intellectual'. They were on 'God in Science', or 'Belgium; its People, Architecture, Painting and

Religion', or 'Israel in Egypt – Monumental Testimonies to the Pentateuch'. They were also highly polemical and George Eliot levelled at Cumming the sort of accusation which was repeatedly aimed at the Y.M.C.A. 'Dr. Cumming's infidel is a man who, because his life is vicious, tries to convince himself that there is no God, and that Christianity is an imposture, but who is all the while secretly conscious that he is opposing the truth, and cannot help "letting out" admissions that the Bible is the Book of God".'[114] Eliot was not prepared to allow Dr. Cumming his fool's paradise.

If Cumming was intellectually too suited to the aspirations of the Y.M.C.A., in other respects he was ideal. He concerned himself with Ragged Schools and kindred philanthropies and among his chapel's organizations was a Young Men's Mutual Improvement Society. On 2 July 1844, two days before Williams and his friends introduced fresh rules for their association, a correspondent, H. J. Fineard, forwarded a copy of 'the Rules of a Society . . . of which I was a member, thinking they may be useful to your committee in drawing up Rules'. The Society was that attached to Crown Court.[115]

James Hamilton, Cumming's fellow Scot and Presbyterian, was a more representative figure. He had three great advantages. He was a young man (only seven years older than George Williams), he was new to London (completing his first full year there in 1842), and he came to a charge which lay open either to revival or catastrophe. Regent Square Presbyterian Church lay on the opposite edge of Bloomsbury to Crown Court. If it lacked Crown Court's distinction, it possessed more than its share of notoriety. It had been Edward Irving's church and Irving bequeathed an impossible legacy. There was, moreover, a fresh cause for concern to Presbyterians in the 1840s. In 1843 the Established Church of Scotland underwent disruption. English Dissenters watched in delight and admiration as the most revered men in the Kirk followed the example of the saints of 1662 and seceded from the establishment. It was inevitable that the disruption should find an echo amongst the few Presbyterian congregations to be found in England. James Hamilton led Regent Square into the ranks of the seceders, to the vocal annoyance of Cumming of Crown Court.

Hamilton must be ranked among the personalities of the Victorian pulpit. By the end of 1842 he had so revived his church that 300 communicants were on the roll.[116] But he was more than a leader for exiled Scotsmen; he was a man of theological weight and scientific interests, combining both in his Exeter Hall lectures.* He was an intimate friend of Baptist Noel, and both men knew the uncertainty and the notoriety of secession. And Hamilton was attractive to young men. In September 1841, barely arrived in London, he formed at his house a Young Men's Society.[117] It was most probably a typical mutual improvement society,[118] but it was a remarkably successful one for it celebrated its jubilee in 1891. It was surely this society which led Hamilton into Y.M.C.A. circles.

He was not a long-lived man, and when he died in 1867 he was only in his early fifties. But it is pleasant to find that in the Jubilee year of 1894, three years after the Jubilee of Hamilton's own society, George Williams noted in his diary a Sunday evening visit to Regent Square.[119] He was not unmindful of his debts.

Notes

1. *King's Weigh House Church Book 1794–1867.*
2. Quoted in Elaine Kaye, *The King's Weigh House Church*, 1968, p. 64.
3. ibid., p. 71.
4. E. Hodder, *The Life of Samuel Morley*, 1887, p. 363.
5. E. Paxton Hood, *Thomas Binney: His Mind, Life and Opinions*, 1874, p. 1.
6. H. Allon, ed., *Sermons preached in the King's Weigh-House Chapel, London 1829–1869 by T. Binney, LL.D.*, 2nd Series, 1875.
7. Hood, op. cit., p. vi.
8. ibid., p. 201.
9. Allon, op. cit., p. xvi.
10. *Church Book 1794–1867*, op. cit.
11. Hood, *op. cit.*, p. 269.
12. ibid., p. 306.
13. Hood, op. cit., p. 168, et seq.
14. *7th Annual Report 1851–1852*, pp. 29–30.
15. Hood, op. cit., p. 300.
16. ibid., p. 280.
17. Hood, op. cit., p. 121.
18. ibid., pp. 215–216.
19. *Congregational Year Book*, 1848, p. 9.

* He chose softer titles than Cumming: 'The Cedar and the Palm', 'The Field and the Garden', 'The Lily of the Valley and the Glory of Lebanon', all in 1845-6.

20. ibid., p. 8.
21. Hodder, op. cit., *passim*, especially pp. 70, 84 et seq., 166, 275.
22. *King's Weigh House Pew Rent Roll 1855-1859.*
23. Helen Caroline Colman, *Jeremiah James Colman* priv., 1905 p. 135.
24. Hood, op. cit., pp. 117–18.
25. ibid., pp. 44–5.
26. ibid., p. 49.
27. ibid., p. 60.
28. H. Davies, *Worship and Theology in England from Newman to Martineau, 1850-1900* (O.U.P., 1962) p. 10.
29. Allon, op. cit., p. xliv.
30. Hood, op. cit., p. 159.
31. ibid., p. 6.
32. ibid., p. 156.
33. ibid., p. 84.
34. Allon, op. cit., liii-liv.
35. Hood, op. cit., p. 86.
36. E. Hodder, *The Life and Work of the 7th Earl of Shaftesbury K.G.*, 1886, vol. II, p. 438: for 13 May 1853.
37. Allon, op. cit., p. xxix et seq; Hood, op. cit., p. 19 et seq; Elaine Kaye op. cit., p. 66 et seq.
38. Hodder, *Morley*, op. cit., p. 275.
39. ibid., p. 362.
40. Elaine Kaye, op. cit., p. 74.
41. Hood, op. cit., pp. 122–3.
42. ibid., pp. 297–8.
43. E. Hodder, op. cit., p. 64. Binney's brother in law, the Revd. Josiah Viney, said this of him.
44. J. R. Leifchild, *John Leifchild D.D.* (Jackson, Walford and *Hodder* of Paternoster Row, 1863) p. 108.
45. *The First Annual Report*, 1846.
46. *Congregational Year Book*, 1894, pp. 229–30.
47. Leifchild, op. cit., pp. 260–72.
48. ibid., frontispiece, from a portrait drawn in 1854. Leifchild, unlike Binney, sported gown and Geneva bands.
49. Leifchild, op. cit., p. 177.
50. ibid., pp. 251–2.
51. Newman Hall, *An Autobiography*, 1898, p. 46.
52. *Congregational Year Book*, 1863, pp. 236–7; Leifchild, op. cit., p. 259.
53. E. Baines, *The Life of Edward Baines*, 1851, p. 288.
54. Leifchild, op. cit., p. 199.
55. Allon, op. cit., p. lvii.
56. Leifchild, op. cit., p. 42. The speaker was William Jay of Bath.

57. ibid., p. 209; p. 201.
58. A. & C. Reed, *Memoirs of Andrew Reed D.D.*, 1863, p. 152.
59. Leifchild, op. cit., p. 58.
60. ibid., pp. 207–8.
61. ibid., p. 200.
62. ibid., p. 182.
63. ibid., p. 202.
64. ibid., p. 201.
65. ibid., p. 303.
66. ibid., p. 249.
67. George Eliot, *Essays and Leaves from a Note-Book*, 1884, p. 145. This essay was originally published as 'Evangelical Teaching: Dr. Cumming', *Westminster Review*, 1855.
68. On 'Sir T. F. Buxton: A Study for Young Men' in the session 1848–9; 'Authorship', 1853–4.
69. Hodder, *Morley*, op. cit., p. 85.
70. Paxton Hood, op. cit., pp. 176 et seq. Two of his four sons settled in Australia.
71. B. Senior, *A Hundred Years at Surrey Chapel*, 1892, pp. 41–5.
72. Williams's *Diary*, 26 December 1843.
73. *Christ Church Westminster Bridge Road, Its Services and Institutions: with Reports for 1896*, 1897, p. 8. *Surrey Chapel: Its Services and Institutions; with Reports for the Year Ending September 1847*, 1847, p. 24.
74. *Surrey Chapel Report*, op. cit., 1847, p. 12.
75. ibid., p. 4.
76. Williams's *Diary*, 3 September 1843; 8 October 1843.
77. Valantine's *Diary*, 8 January 1843; 11 September 1843.
78. E. Beaumont to G. Williams, 22 October 1859 (?): copy, Nat. Council MSS.
79. *Surrey Chapel Report*, 1856, p. 3; *Surrey Chapel Report* 1860, p. 37.
80. *Surrey Chapel Report*, 1847, p. 39; John Campbell, *Memoirs of David Nasmith*, 1844, p. 465; *Surrey Chapel Sunday School Minute Book, 1828–1844*, 27 May 1844 (when the book was proposed), 17 June 1844 (when it was ordered).
81. Valantine's *Diary*, 25 December 1844.
82. This would appear to be the meeting specified in an undated Memorandum by J. C. Symons: copy, Nat. Council MSS.
83. Valantine's *Diary*, 25 December 1844.
84. B. Senior, op. cit., pp. 158–63.
85. Williams's *Diary*, 22 October 1843.
86. Valantine's *Diary*, 29 October 1843.
87. See I. Stock, *William Hale White (Mark Rutherford): A Critical Study*, 1956, pp. 44–5; 239.

88. J. E. Hodder Williams, *The Life of Sir George Williams*, 1906, p. 38.
89. 'Mark Rutherford', *The Revolution in Tanner's Lane*, 1893, 10th impression 1923, p. 101.
90. 'Mark Rutherford', *Catharine Furze*, 7th ed., n.d., p. 114.
91. Williams's *Diary*, 26 March 1843; Valantine's *Diary*, 18 June 1843.
92. *34th Annual Report 1878–9*, p. 29.
93. *Annual Report of the Somerset Congregational Union*, 1896, p. 52.
94. *18th Annual Report*, 1862; Ronald Taylor, *150 Years Not Out*, n.d., *c.* 1949; *Union Chapel: The Story of a Hundred Years*, 1899, *passim.* Allon's Exeter Hall lectures included two on Church Music and one on Palissy the Potter.
95. *Congregational Year Book*, 1894, pp. 229–30; J. Campbell, op. cit., pp. 386–7.
96. Williams's *Diary*, 19 May 1843.
97. ibid., 8 January 1843.
98. Valantine's *Diary*, 17 September 1843; 11 September 1843; 26 February 1843; Williams's *Diary*, 26 February 1843.
99. (C. H. Spurgeon) *C. H. Spurgeon: The Early Years 1834–1859*, 1962, p. 279. This is the revised edition of his autobiography, first published 1897–1900.
100. Hodder, *Morley*, op. cit., p. 212.
101. W. Brock, 'The Common Origins of the Human Race', *Exeter Hall Lectures 1848–49*, esp. p. 130. It was delivered on 12 December 1848; his other lectures included 'Daniel as a Model for Young Men' 1850–1; 'Young Men for the Age' 1852–3; 'Mercantile Morality' 1855–6; C. M. Birrell, *The Life of William Brock DD*, 1878, p. 190.
102. *7th Annual Report 1851–52*, esp. pp. 10–13.
103. The dedication was dated 3 May 1844; J. Campbell, *Memoirs of David Nasmith*, 1844, p. iv.
104. Valantine's *Diary*, 9 March 1843.
105. Noel to Nasmith 8 April 1835, Campbell, op. cit., pp. 303–4.
106. H. Allon, *Sermons Preached in the King's Weigh House*, 2nd series, 1875, p. xxxiii. He was also lecturing to the Y.M.C.A. He gave 'The History of the Formation of the Free Church of the Canton de Vaud' in the session 1847–8, while still an Anglican; 'The Church and the World' 1848–9; 'A Revival of Religion' 1850–1.
107. W. E. Shipton, *The Young Men's Christian Association in London . . . A Report Presented to the Conference of Young Men's Christian Associations, held in Paris in August 1855*, p. 8.
108. Williams's *Diary*, 3 January 1843; 10 September 1843; Valantine's *Diary*, 9 March 1843.
109. Valantine's *Diary*, 1 November 1843.

110. ibid., 24 September 1843.
111. C. M. Davies, *Orthodox London*, Series II, 1875, p. 321.
112. For John Cumming 1807–1881, see *D.N.B.*
113. George Eliot, *Essays and Leaves from a Note Book*, 1884, pp. 152–4.
114. ibid., p. 165.
115. Copy, Nat. Council MSS.
116. J. Hair, *Regent Square*, 1899, p. 148.
117. Hair, op. cit., p. 149.
118. T. H. Tarlton to G. Williams, 16 May 1883, Nat. Council MSS.
119. Williams's *Diary*, 9 September 1894.

CHAPTER IV

The Metropolitan Draper's World

The pulpit ministrations of John Leifchild and Thomas Binney offered spiritual food but George Williams's material life depended on the drapery trade. The trade was arduous and exciting and it posed the problem which faced all converted men. As far as young drapers were concerned, Finney had thus expressed it: 'Christian lady have you never doubted whether it be lawful to copy the extravagant fashions of the day, brought from foreign countries and from places which it would be shame even to name? And if you doubt and do it you are condemned, and must repent of your sin or you will be lost for ever'.[1] Could what was denied the Christian lady be permitted to the assistant who served her? Williams was not given to reconciling the irreconcilable and he simply, manfully, made the best of both worlds, as Binney taught rather more helpfully than Finney.

Victorian drapery was a world where the best could be made. A month after George Williams's death there was a Prime Minister, Campbell Bannerman, whose personal fortune derived from the trade.* It was one of the most typical, and least known, of Victorian success stories. The student of nineteenth-century Nonconformity cannot fail to be impressed at the number of drapers prominent on membership rolls, and at the way they prospered. However small, each town had its Mr. Holmes who was, as often as not, a Dissenter. Drapery became an escape route for aspiring young Dissenters whom means or intellect or luck debarred from the more usual opening in the ministry or even the professions. It was a softening, almost a civilizing, influence while remaining a fiercely competitive business.

* He had been a partner in his family's Glasgow clothing firm until 1868, when he entered politics. 'Sir Henry Campbell-Bannerman', *Dictionary of National Biography*.

A successful draper could not fail to become a deacon, although if his trade really enticed the nobility and gentry whose patronage he claimed, it was better to conform to the Established Church.

At the head of the trade, although he can hardly be called a *draper*, towered Samuel Morley the mainstay of them all, the great manufacturer of shirts, stockings and other garments. The Morley business house originated in the late eighteenth century. Samuel Morley was already a rich man when, with two brothers and a cousin, he assumed effectual command of the business in the early 1840s. By the time of his death in 1886 Morley ruled an empire which was the largest of its kind in the textile industry. His seven midland factories employed, directly or indirectly, 8,000 hands.[2] The business of his London warehouses in Wood Street, Cheapside, was reflected in a mail second only to that dealt with by the Prudential Assurance Company.[*] A clerkship at Morley's was a dream for the sons of all pious widows in straitened circumstances.

Morley was in the exhilarating position of being an industrialist on a new scale. He was an employer of the second generation who was yet close enough to his origins for paternalism to make sense. He exercised his responsibility with the utmost care and Morley's remained a family business, at times using old techniques for purely sentimental reasons while yet pioneering benefits for its employees and consolidating its reputation. Only an established firm sure of its royal patronage could name one corset after the Princess of Wales and produce another, 'French wove', which was pleasantly frilly and lacy.[†]

Morley's sense of responsibility, with that of his retiring brother John, revealed itself in his London warehouses in the closest liaison with the Y.M.C.A. His employees lived on the premises, so he endowed them with a library and reading room, parlours and a dining room. He encouraged a multiplicity of improvement societies. He did not prevent them from drinking, but he did object to them being Roman Catholics. He gave them holidays and a sense of security not easily found elsewhere. Until 1865 he paid his young men personally.[3]

---

[*] It averaged 2,000 letters daily by first post alone, E. Hodder, *The Life of Samuel Morley*, 1887, p. 195.

[†] This was in the 1870s. Or the purchaser might prefer the black Ventnor or the formidable Phellopektos Grand Duchess. Alison Adburgham, *Shops and Shopping 1800–1914*, 1964, pp. 131–2.

Morley was a giant, but he was unique neither in his success nor his sense of duty, and he had his imitators within the world of drapery proper. In the nature of things it was inevitable that drapers should outnumber other piously concerned businessmen in their subscriptions to the Y.M.C.A., and it is pleasant to find in the lists published with each report from the late 1840s the names of Redmayne, Swan and Edgar, later of Debenham and Freebody, Dickins and Jones, Lewis and Allenby, as well as Crosse and Blackwell, Fortnum and Mason and, inevitably, W. H. Smith. It seemed that the *Saturday Review* was correct in its assertion that 'philanthropy seems especially affected by drapers; they take to it as naturally as shoemakers and tailors take to politics.'[4] This was the world of Hitchcock, Rogers.

When George Williams died, the press, with the hyperbole proper to the occasion, referred frequently to the 'old-established' nature of his firm. Doubtless its reputation for judicious conservatism contributed to this and the image was carefully fostered, 'the traditional atmosphere of the merchant prince's establishment has always pervaded the house, this conception of the nobility of commerce has been the basis of all their work'.[5] They were certainly a relatively old firm although the date now accepted by them as the earliest one when they were ascertainably in business is 1829, which is necessarily arbitrary.* A contemporary engraving shows Ludgate House, No. 1 St. Paul's Churchyard, the retail premises of F. Rogers and Co, and an engraving of some six years later at, or just before, the removal to No. 72, shows the rather grandly classical premises of Hitchcock and Rogers, a building with large plate-glass windows on the ground floor and pilasters, entablature and nicely proportioned upper windows.[6]

Frederick Rogers is a shadowy character who retired in 1843 and George Hitchcock, a young man whose earlier life is hardly less shadowy, was the architect of the house's grandeur and assurance. It is not known when he entered into partnership with Rogers. It is possible, since he had been in London from 1827, that he was already concerned with a wholesale business in Watling Street which later joined with the house in St. Paul's Churchyard.[7] What is certain is that by 1841 Hitchcock, Rogers was a reputable business and that George Hitchcock at the head of nearly 150 assistants was a pushing,

* The firm's records perished in the Second World War. The date given by Walden (1835) (see note 5) is certainly too late.

enlightened and (save in the eyes of the truly pious) responsible employer who fitted naturally and prominently into the new world of fashionable wholesale and retail drapery.

Because it was a new world it was a harsh one. It would take more than the enlightenment of intelligent business principals to alter the facts and assumptions of Victorian *laissez-faire* life. The conditions in which most drapers' assistants worked were appalling. They were so partly because good but unreflecting businessmen had nothing to measure them against, partly because these conditions were only a temporary stage for most aspiring apprentices and partly because current economic theory meant that even the simplest improvement cut across accepted conventions in such a way as to suggest madness in the reformer. Since the source of the mill-owner's, or shopkeeper's, profit lay in the last hour, how could one reduce the number of hours worked, even if common humanity told one that the work was grindingly hard? In a new and competitive trade, dependent on the whims of fashion and the credit of the fashionable and reliant on inadequate capital, how could a man afford to experiment in the name of a misleading humanity? And given the squalor and violence of London life which was of a scale quite new to Englishmen, how could a responsible employer allow yet more leisure to lusty and overgrown boys of assistants? The stops in the minds of these self-made men were too large, and for even the most humane the greatest concessions were strict. 'Men employees are given one evening each week for courting purposes, and two if they go to prayer-meeting regularly.'[8] Long after less hours, along with other benefits, had been accepted as desirable in principle, it remained usual for a girl employee of Selincourt and Colman to start work at 5 a.m. and even at Morley's, where latterly the employees did not work after 5 p.m. in the winter months, it was accepted that the hours must be harder in the busy season.* *Kipps*, which publicized the shop assistants' trials as remembered by H. G. Wells from his experiences of the 1880s before the Act of 1886 improved matters, appeared in 1905 which was the year of Williams's death.

* Alison Adburgham, op. cit., pp. 125–6, E. Hodder, *Morley*, op. cit., p. 202. From the 1850s the wholesale firm of Selincourt and Colman pioneered a wide range of ready-to-wear garments, their waterproof cloaks aptly named after seaside resorts. Their Cannon Street premises were close to the London headquarters of J. and J. Colman. The Selincourts were a family long attached to the Westminster Chapel, a Congregational Chapel friendly to the Y.M.C.A. from the Association's earliest days.

Holmes of Bridgwater and Hitchcock of St. Paul's Churchyard were admirable employers. Yet Hodder Williams gives an account of George Williams's shop assistant days which is corroborated elsewhere. The living-in system which had a most respectable history and could have been one of the blessings of paternalism (as perhaps it was, at Morley's) became intolerable in the distorted conditions of early Victorian London. The Y.M.C.A's. ninth report stated the matter bluntly: 'whatever may be the necessities of business, the fact that large numbers of Young Men thus live together, frequently in compelled celibacy, operates with melancholy effect on moral character and habit.'[9] George Hitchcock, speaking later in 1854 at the opening of the Aldersgate buildings, recalled his own experiences in the 1820s and 1830s:

'Young men in the large houses, for they were worse than the small ones, were herded together, ten or fifteen in a room, at night. They were literally driven from the shop to their beds, and from their beds to the shop, by a person called a shopwalker. There was no sitting room, no social comfort, no library; they remained until they were taken ill, then they were discharged at a moment's notice: away they went, many of them to the workhouse, and numbers used to die prematurely.'[10]

Although George Williams greatly benefited from what George Hitchcock had learned, there is enough evidence in his diary that what Hitchcock endured in the 1830s still obtained in the 1840s. The hours and conditions at St. Paul's Churchyard were spartan. The dormitories seldom had more than three beds in them, but each bed had two occupants. The hours were from 7 a.m. to 9 p.m. (an hour earlier in the winter) with barely a break for meals, but business did not cease the moment the shop closed and the prompt bolting of the street doors at 11 p.m. left the minimal time for private recreation.

Hodder Williams was not original but neither was he exaggerating in his assertion that outside business hours the only relaxations were in drinking, smoking and gambling at the Goose and Gridiron next door in the Churchyard, or whoring in the pleasure gardens. As he put it, it was an elemental world where swearing was the only acceptable conversation and which allowed you only to be immoral or immorally dull. Yet equally there was enough competition and excitement for it really to be 'the day of the Young Man'.[11] Only so unredeemed an atmosphere could foster the contrary enthusiasm needed for a lasting, successful Y.M.C.A. Damnation is twin to salvation, as every saved man knows, and George Williams was accurate in his belief that in the London of his young manhood, a youth's first day determined where he was to spend eternity.[12] Despite Thomas Binney's protestations, the shop assistants' condition could allow no middle way. An understanding of this made the Y.M.C.A. possible. Mercifully, when a middle way later became desirable, Williams for all his qualms did not oppose it. This forbearance saved the Y.M.C.A.

Drapers' assistants had one inestimable advantage over other victims of the age – there was always the prospect of a shop of their own. Drapers, being pretentious shopkeepers, could expect large premiums from their apprentices, which presupposed in them a certain financial backing. George Williams had that backing. His initial salary in London was £40 a year (the pittance traditionally enjoyed by the village pastor) yet apparently there quickly arose the possibility that he might return to Bridgwater to buy Holmes's business.* Williams had perhaps inherited a small sum from his father, very likely at the suggestion of his draper brother, but the fact that he remained in London indicates that the prospects were both promising and rapid for an ambitious young man with some backing and more luck. This was the whole attraction of the drapery trade.

The expansion of the trade in the forty years before Williams came to London had been particularly rapid and by 1841 despite competition from Regent Street and other western thoroughfares, St. Paul's Churchyard was at its height as the hub of the drapery business, offering a sophistication and even a brilliance which compensated for temporary hardship. Although the Churchyard was the centre of the wholesale side, retail trade also flourished and it was this which added the façade and the panache. Hitchcock, Rogers at Nos. 72–74, were among the more established businesses. In the 1830s a touch of fashionable and continental femininity was provided at No. 71 by the paper-pattern shop of Mrs. Smith and the Parisian Mme. La

---

* J. E. Hodder Williams, *The Life of Sir George Williams*, 1906, pp. 46, 50. This is corroborated by the fact that Holmes disappears from the poll books from 1841 – he was 'Disqualified from voting through change of residence'. By 1852, the Holmes family had returned to Bridgwater as drapers. I am indebted to the Bridgwater Borough Librarian for this information.

Poulli.* From the early 1840s, the wholly retail firm of Nicholson's (Hitchcock's rivals of longest standing) was at Nos. 50–54.[13] Rather later, when the West End had replaced St. Paul's as the centre of retail fashion, the houses of Hitchcock, Nicholson and James Spence (of Nos. 76–79) retained a long-established clientele which was more than merely genteel. Safety had perhaps replaced the extremes of fashion but complete and enviable respectability remained. St. Paul's Churchyard was in fact close enough to Cannon Street and Black-friars Railway Stations, and even to Charing Cross and Liverpool Street, to attract the propertied ladies of Bromley, Chislehurst, Buckhurst Hill, Woodford and the other expanding villages, long after their sisters in Kensington and Bayswater had been lured else-where.

The dynamism of drapery was readily apparent. It was a common-place that drapers' shops were foremost in improving and beautifying their premises. In particular, drapers had incorporated two eye-catching advances – plate-glass and gas lighting. Shops at St. Paul's whose fronts were an 'uninterrupted mass of glass'[14] were a vast advance on the usual run of ill-lit, cavernous premises. Inevitably, plate-glass demanded elegant and frequently changed displays which might attract the shopper and lure her with the prospects of greater delights inside. Plate-glass windows were large windows, large win-dows suggested larger shops, and larger shops demanded an intricate, efficient, and genteel service within. This was a secret of Hitchcock's success. Gas lighting was no less important. A mode of lighting 'by which the products of combustion are given off in the street, instead of being left to soil the goods in the window: the lamps . . . fixed outside the shops, with a reflector so placed as to throw down a strong light upon the commodities in the window,'[15] was a godsend in an ill-lit city where shops usually remained open into the evening. It did more than anything else to thrust the elegance and display of these up-to-date shops into the streets themselves.

Another and less obvious factor indicates the dynamism of the trade. This was the drapers' equivalent of what has already been glimpsed in the world of the Dissenting minister – the freshness and self-sufficiency of self-made men balanced by a host of connexions. It was almost a freemasonry. George Hitchcock was a Devon man, George Williams was from Somerset. So was John Snelgrove, six

* They charged their girl assistants a premium of ten guineas, see Alison Adburgham, op. cit., pp. 39–40.

years Williams's senior, who had arrived in London rather earlier and whose rise to a partnership in what became Marshall and Snelgrove, was slightly more rapid. Snelgrove was a man of similar interests to Williams. They were both devout, benevolent, retiring men, sharing a liking for Torquay. It is pleasant to find Williams noting in Jubilee year that Snelgrove gave him £250 for the beloved movement.* John Lewis, a generation or so later, was another Somerset lad.[16]

In contrast, Cambridge's leading draper, Robert Sayle, had graduated from an apprenticeship in St. Paul's Churchyard. His career is a copy-book illustration of the position which Victorian drapers occupied.[17] He was five years older than George Williams, the son of a gentleman farmer of Southery, in Norfolk. His education at Ely, and his early prospects as a solicitor, followed naturally from his family's standing. In fact he was not articled to a solicitor and from May 1838 to February 1840 he was an apprentice at Hitchcock, Rogers of St. Paul's Churchyard. Sayle left this for his own business in Cambridge, the money for which had been provided by his father, and for the next forty years he was prominent in Cambridge's philanthropic and religious life. Like Williams, he lived on the borderland between Church and Chapel, giving the Cambridge Wesleyans the status already held by Baptists and Congregationalists.† Sayle's money was generously spent in the cause of education and in the 1870s he was, with George Williams, a guarantor of the newly-built Cambridge Y.M.C.A., and a sponsor of the neighbouring Improved Industrial Dwellings.

Robert Sayle was by no means unique among drapers in eastern England, and King's Lynn's foremost draper, Alfred Jermyn, illus-

---

* *Diary*, 17 April 1894. On 18 April, Williams noted, 'Saw Marshall and Debenham both promised to consider.' Williams and Snelgrove left similar fortunes of over £200,000, but Snelgrove lived in greater opulence at 23 Kensington Palace Gardens. He died aged 87 in December 1903. *The Times*, 8 December 1903; 9 February 1904; Alison Adburgham, op. cit., p. 45.

† Miss Sieveking, the historian of Robert Sayle and Co., states that Sayle was an Anglican, worshipping at Great St. Andrews Church. Frank Tice, *The History of Methodism in Cambridge*, 1966, *passim.*, esp. p. 133, assumes that Sayle was a Wesleyan. Certainly his benevolence would have been remarkable coming from a non-Methodist at a time of increasing rivalry between Church and Dissent. The answer may lie in Sayle's Norfolk origins where the boundary between Church and Wesleyanism was easily blurred. At Southery he subscribed with equal impartiality to Church and Chapel. Sayle died in 1883.

trates further the trading web on which the Y.M.C.A., for example, could rely and prosper. In October 1894, as part of the Jubilee commemoration, George Williams visited Norfolk. He dined and slept with the Colmans at Carrow House and then he went to King's Lynn where his host was Alfred Jermyn. Williams enjoyed a 'real good time' and his hosts later declared that 'no one ever entered their house who showed greater Christian courtesy than did this prince of philanthropy'. Jermyn was no less representative than Robert Sayle, prominent in the politics of his town, prosperous in its business, and prolific in its philanthropies. He was a Wesleyan whose connexions with the Y.M.C.A. dated from the 1860s and his days in London when, searching for a situation, George Williams helped him.[18]

The dynamism of the trade was reflected in another way. Drapery's competitiveness both caused and came from this dynamism, and yet the trade remained a conservative one. It seemed to be more competitive than other businesses partly because of the fickleness of fashion, and partly because of the impact of the cotton industry. There was little showy in woollens, and silks were too expensive for close competition. But cottons were both comparatively cheap and showy. They were, therefore, fashionable and competitive. The relative cheapness of cotton manufacture created a demand which clamoured for further production. 'The mills, the labour, the capital employed in this manufacture have led to so large a production that the manufacturer is anxious to "do business" in any quarter, and this anxiety leads to a constant increase in the number of retail shops.'[19] One result of this as far as London was concerned, was a continuous removal to the West End, pursuing respectability at its very doors.

Because it was a trade whose life-blood was respectability, it was a conservative trade. I. and R. Morley achieved its accolade when Queen Victoria approved their stockings. Only then might it progress to frilly French corsetry. No reputable retail firm could be without its mourning warehouse, but many of the utmost respectability stocked the most delicate and alluring of mourning mauves. Perhaps it was because the dividing line between the acceptable and the improper was so slight that the trade was so insistent on good order. Hitchcock's sought to attract a county, or at least a Home County, connexion; but *ladies* never shopped alone and then only at certain hours. It was therefore important that ladies be served by a profusion of young men who were gentlemanly without being gentlemen. Assistants must speak well and dress well. At Hitchcock's they must wear black broadcloth coats and white ties and be clean shaven. In the relatively few retail establishments where women were employed a genteel 'morning costume' was required.[20] Further cultivation was not expected. Somewhat earlier and in a rather different context, Francis Place, the Charing Cross tailor and political wire-puller extraordinary, had noted of his customers:

> 'had these persons been told that I had never read a book, that I was ignorant of everything but my own business, that I sotted in a public house, they would not have made the least objection to me. I should have been a "fellow" beneath them, and they would have patronized me; but . . . to accumulate books, and to be supposed to know something of their content, and seek for friends, too, among literary and scientific men, was putting myself on an equality with themselves, if not indeed assuming a superiority; it was an abominable offence in a tailor'.[21]

It was more than enough that young people 'in business' should be content simply to display in the best manner 'the innumerable whim-whams and fribble-frabbles of fashion'.[22]

Real as this conservatism was – and if snobbery is the perquisite of those with least cause for it then it was surely born on the wrong side of the draper's counter – it yet had unpredictable results. Larger shops were a stage towards department stores where the comforts of shopping went far beyond mere counter service. It was inevitable that these shops, catering for the wants of women through their husbands' pockets, should contribute gently but persistently to the independence of women.[23] It was a long process, but George Williams's life was longer.

Each of these trends is important in contributing to an understanding of the life of Williams. His faith was at once conservative and freshly aggressive, nurtured in a certain bracing inferiority. Politically he tended no less to the conservative, although only an imperial vision could have encompassed the unforeseen international growth of his association. As a businessman Williams was equally ambivalent. His business developed rapidly and he ensured that it developed widely. It also developed circumspectly. There was to be no move to the West End. Instead the future was to lie in the socially preferable wholesale trade whose profits were more assured, if less spectacular. And for an undoubtedly aggressive and missionary agency, the Y.M.C.A. was usually found on the safer side and its young men were ideally those of the lower middle-class – gentlemanly but not gentlemen.

In the *Weekly True Sun* for Sunday, 30 April 1837, an elaborate notice advertised the removal to new and spacious premises of Hitchcock and Rogers. The new establishment displaced a publisher, a bookseller, the residence of the librarian of St. Paul's School, and a trunk-maker. The intention was to house on one site a wholesale and a retail business, but there were wider implications in the advertisement. It displayed that mixture of progress and respectability, and unless it unduly exaggerated it foreshadowed the department stores of later in the century. A lady should have all her needs satisfied in the one establishment: 'The NOBILITY AND PUBLIC GENERALLY as well as COUNTRY MILLINERS in particular, have often expressed their regret that at no one Establishment in the Metropolis could they procure all that they desire in useful and ornamental apparel.'

Consequently, Hitchcock and Rogers promised twelve departments from the silk mercery and haberdashery for which they were already noted, through jewellery and perfumery, French flowers, horlogerie and fancy porcelain, to boys' caps and 'French and German Manufactures, both useful and ornamental, adapted either for the Work Table, Toilet, or Drawing Room, and comprising some of the most curious and valuable novelties ever imported into this country'.

The nobility, general public and country milliners were further informed of 'a Parisian Milliner who will be in constant attendance to receive orders, and to effect any alterations which ladies may suggest'. They were assured that 'from the British and foreign talent engaged in this department, Hitchcock Rogers confidently anticipate their periodical display of FANCY BONNETS, TURBANS, etc., will be equal to any yet exhibited in London'. It seemed that the needlework of the baby linen was 'of a very curious description' and it was announced that the sautoirs, sachets, canzous and embroidered mantillas comprised 'the most splendid collection ever exhibited in one establishment'. The list continues – it includes ostrich plumes and china, footwear and writing desks, cravats and mirrors and fans. 'The Jewellery . . . will be found to combine elegance with extreme economy'; and for more intimate matters 'The oils, Extracts, and Cosmetiques, etc, etc, are purchased from a Parisian House of high character, and as the Proprietors have received a guarantee for their purity and excellence, they feel no hesitation in strongly recommending them. . . .'

The proprietors indeed spared no pains in reassuring their customers. In the silk and linen departments they promised their personal attention, the carpets and furnishings were to be 'managed by competent persons', no ladies were to be 'annoyed by being repeatedly solicited to purchase', neither was there to be any deviation from the price asked. Hitchcock, Rogers was not a bazaar and it was not in a provincial town – it was almost another home.

Clearly, manliness was the more to be pursued in so feminine an atmosphere and the background to this gentility – the long hours, the cramped bedrooms, the constricted young men reading the sternly disapproving works of Finney, and weekly sampling the headier wares of Binney – affords an uncomfortable and suggestive contrast.

In 1905 the *Schoolmaster* rather hopefully saw a 'quiet and serene romance' in George Williams's career.[24] It was neither quiet nor serene although it was romantic. That it seemed so was the ultimate tribute to an eminently successful draper.

The Third Annual Report for 1847 of the London Y.M.C.A. contained correspondence received from associated business houses. One gave a dismal account of a commercial London in which the hours of work had already improved, which made the moral void in the great city all the more apparent. The Association's informant had received their tract of *Life*, a pamphlet addressed to 'intelligent and active minds', and this emboldened him to write incoherently:

'a more reckless house of young men . . . is not to be found in the city of London. During dinner, tea, and supper-time, nothing but obscene language is going on; such as scenes in brothels, night-brawls, etc, too disgusting to commit to paper, and in the presence of *junior hands and apprentices*. To what end must this young generation come? I shudder at the idea! I am writing these lines within the hearing of the latter, playing cards – not for pleasure, no! but for a halfpenny the game, swearing at the top of their voices, and calling each other cheats.'

In such a context any later suspicion of innocent recreation is understandable. How could any form of recreation be innocent in a house whose uncaring principals 'indulge them with late nights for the purpose of going to theatres. Yes! and worse than theatres, those *Casinos*, where they dance and mix with the unfortunates!

'Warehouses close now at six o'clock p.m., and the remaining five hours, until eleven, should be quite enough for their debaucheries without keeping open until twelve or one in the morning, and some of them do not appear until the following day ... We sometimes see the worst characters placed in the most important situations in the large houses, as buyers and head salesmen, and, strange to say, they are the most *pushing* heads and hardest workers. But, mind you, only for a time – for a year or two.'[25]

This is the epitome of George Williams's London – the certainty of the writer, the degradation of his subject, the impossibility of a middle way, and yet the prospect of better things to come. It sets the problem which Williams felt concerned to solve. Ironically the problem, intractable as it seemed and terrible as it was, was already changing. London had been a perplexing and frightening phenomenon at least since Tudor times. From the late eighteenth century its intensity had increased beyond all understanding. If it was inconceivable for drapers to soften the working conditions of their employees, how much less conceivable was it for vestrymen and liverymen to regulate their living conditions. The changes in urban government caused by the Municipal Corporations Act of 1835 (one of the most far-reaching measures of that moderately but insistently reforming decade) by-passed the metropolis. London, apart from the City, was under-represented in Parliament and it was grossly under-governed. Despite gentle and desultory tinkering it was to remain so until the institution of the London County Council in 1889. Between the last decade of the eighteenth century and the last of the nineteenth century the population of the city and its suburbs had risen from over one million to over seven million.

The influx of thousands of young men to the capital was too obvious to be ignored or dismissed, least of all by one so newly-conscious of individual souls as George Williams, who was himself part of the problem. It was this influx of pushing, black-coated youths which distorted the living-in system and which Williams sought to counteract. But the growth of suburbs meant that the short-term problem within the City, which was Williams's immediate concern, was soon to be replaced. In the twenty years after 1851 (the year in which the Y.M.C.A. really 'found' itself) the resident population of the City dropped from 128,000 to 75,000. Already by 1863 one correspondent could report, with a note of despair because the new situation meant that missionary work was becoming too diffuse, that 'nearly all the Young Men engaged in our house sleep off the premises, and most of them in the suburbs.'[26]

The English suburb with its peculiar snobbery had been born in London. Largely created in the seventeenth century, usually restricted to the rich and aristocratic in the eighteenth century, it had become a middle-class thing by the middle of the nineteenth century. George Williams himself, from the days of his prosperity, kept to Bloomsbury. Woburn and Russell Squares were within easy reach of the City and their dignity and long-established nature, their surprising seclusion and leafiness, gave them a unique charm for the solider classes of business and professional men. Bloomsbury had ceased to be truly aristocratic, but Samuel Morley began his married life in Upper Bedford Place and later Samuel Habershon lived close by. Thomas Binney moved from Southwark to Camden Town and thence to Upper Clapton. Islington was the area favoured by his congregation, Edward Valantine among them. The Leifchilds preferred the purlieus of Regent's Park, rather to westward. George Hitchcock moved from Blackfriars to Norfolk Crescent, where Hyde Park merges politely into Bayswater and Paddington.

Islington, Bloomsbury, and Hyde Park soon saw Y.M.C.A.s as they were all growing districts with flourishing chapels and strongly evangelical Churches. They were all aggressively respectable with the great advantage that their residents included precisely those well-connected and prosperous men without whose help no Victorian philanthropy could survive.

Samuel Morley's residences exemplify this. He had been born in 1809, in Hackney. By 1841 he lived in Bloomsbury. From 1842 he was in Clapton, which had replaced Hackney as Nonconformity's favourite retreat and thence to Stamford Hill which was still in the tradition – the Stamford Hill Congregational Church was the scene of many distinguished Nonconformist funerals, Thomas Binney's among them. Morley's departure to Mayfair in 1870, with a country estate in the heart of Kent, was therefore of considerable social significance and of some advantage to the Y.M.C.A. In no way relinquishing his radical Liberalism or his Nonconformity, Morley had entered the London of the Shaftesburys, Aberdeens, Kinnairds, of the Buxtons and the Hanburys, whose influence was so welcome to the mature Y.M.C.A.

The Association was quickly cherished in these districts, but none of them had the problem of massed young men peculiar to the City in the 1840s which had first attracted George Williams. Their problems were further from the surface.

With the passing of the 1840s, less favoured areas became suburbs. An eastward expansion of almost American rapidity converted first Stratford and then Walthamstow from inexpensively respectable retreats to lower middle-class suburbs and worse. The introduction of cheap workmen's returns intensified this trend. It was just here, some distance from the villas of bountiful subscribers, that the next challenge for the Y.M.C.A. came.

But in 1844 it was the immediate problem of the City which concerned George Williams. Just as St. Paul's Churchyard was a cosmopolitan, fashionable thoroughfare in the 1840s, so it was still possible for the City, extended perhaps to include Finsbury, to be considered as respectably residential. Paxton Hood, speaking of the 1830s, expressed the conclusions which were to be drawn: 'the mighty middle class, from which Dissent is constantly invigorated, lived then within the walls of the City, or within its immediate neighbourhood ... the Independents of London formed a strong and united confederacy'. But between these two significant statements he qualified his conception of a 'mighty middle class', 'especially the young men – clerks, shopkeepers, and others – found their homes there'.[27]

That the numbers of the middle-class were great, was undoubted. 'Taking the Parliamentary Abstract of Population as their authority, the Committee find there is *a greater number of young men*, between the ages of 20 and 30, *living in the Metropolis, than there are in the principal towns of twenty-six Counties in England, including the City of York*. Where is the provision for their immortal souls?'[28] J. C. Symons, describing the origins of the Y.M.C.A. to an Australian audience in 1856, assured them that in 1844 at least 50,000 London shopmen were passing 'their doomed life in cheerless lassitude till they exchange it for an early tomb'.[29] W. E. Shipton, speaking in Paris a year earlier, described a London where in 1844 150,000 young men worked in warehouses and shops, a figure which had risen to 250,000 a decade later.[30] Y.M.C.A. audiences were accustomed to sweeping statements and striking facts. Whether these men worked or lived in London is unimportant, these figures entered association lore and led to fresh advance. What gave such figures an added poignancy was that socially at least these young men were by no means doomed. Their position was merely perilous, and they existed suspended in their Mahomet's coffin between the lower orders and the intelligent classes to whom by rights they belonged. This made Christian action doubly urgent, and to these numbers of men some added the more distressful young women. In 1843 there were, for example, 1,500 milliners over the age of 14 employed in London.[31] Their conditions and their prospects were minimal, yet respectability tinged even them.

The whole question was deeply interesting – there was almost a terrible romance in it. In the midst, oases of faith, stood the Churches and the chapels, and eight o'clock on a Sunday evening when the chapels disgorged their congregations, was a favourite time for pick-pockets. Paxton Hood remembered how Binney preached on London's midnight dissipations when 'quite suddenly, and with his own peculiar force, he exclaimed, "Watchman, what of the night? Watchman, what of the night?"' and his hearers, the rows of young men, visibly thrilled as each pictured the carriages, the drunkards, the confusion, the lights and the dark, and then heard Binney's famous sigh. . . .[32] The young men at least had a certain faculty of imagination. It is among the less expected aspects of George Williams's youth that he felt Byron to be worthy of committing to memory. 'Mark Rutherford', who was also an attender at the City's chapels and whose novels describe unforgettably the greyness of the lowest London respectability, had himself encountered the fascination of Byron and commented, 'not to the prosperous man, a dweller in beautiful scenery, well married to an intelligent wife, is Byron precious, but to the poor wretch, say some City clerk, with an aspiration beyond his desk, who has two rooms in Camberwell.'[33]

For such people it was the easiest thing in the world, and the most terrible, to slide into the degradation which made London notorious in Western Europe. Perhaps the draper's assistants' dream of his own shop made the sharper his knowledge of the rookery tenements behind him. It was the discovery of London's poor which brought Lord Ashley within the orbit of the Y.M.C.A., and it was working among London's poor as well as London's apprentices which cemented the friendship between Williams, Valantine and their associates. If the Y.M.C.A. was a child of the Evangelical Revival and also of the drapery trade, it was at least a godchild of London's need for humanity.

It is not necessary to look beyond Edwin Hodder's *Life* of Shaftesbury for evidence of this. The problem of tenements where exorbitant rents crushed men into poverty whose wages in the provinces would have been ample, but whose work laid them at the mercy of a vast city lacking in cheap transport, had become a permanent feature of London life – 'you will see flowing before each hovel, and within a few feet of it, a broad, black, uncovered drain, exhaling at every point the most unwholesome vapours. If there be not a drain, there is a stagnant pool; touch either with your stick, and the mephitic mass will yield up its poisonous gas like the coruscations of soda-water.'[34] Symons, Williams and Shipton were appalled at the thousands of shopmen. Ashley was no less concerned at London's 30,000 'naked filthy, roaring, lawless and deserted children', who were on a lower level altogether than the merely ordinary poor.* And if the charm of Bloomsbury lay in its being so close to the City and yet so select, it was Ashley who had discovered in 1847 that in Church Lane, Bloomsbury, an average of forty people lived in each dwelling.[35] What was the answer? Road improvement? But where and how were those made homeless in this way to be re-housed? Mr. Cutting's excellently paved New Oxford Street which offered such scope for Craven Chapel, had caused just such an upheaval, and it would be illuminating to discover what resulted from the displacement of Carnaby Market by Craven Chapel itself.

In this London, the Young Man was completely vulnerable, but his case need never be hopeless. This was important for the Y.M.C.A.'s growth and its continued success. For young men at least, life on a knife-edge can be a thrilling experience.

The National Council of Y.M.C.As. possesses a fragment of manuscript, torn, ill-spelt and much amended. It tells a story which clearly had been rounded and improved at many public meetings. It was part of the experience of one of the founder members, Edward Beaumont, like Valantine and Williams a Congregationalist. Beaumont had passed it on to Williams:

'I was standing at my shop door [in The High, Oxford] some little time, since when I saw a shabily dress'd man approach me.

---

* This was in 1848, E. Hodder, *The Life & Work of the 7th Earl of Shaftesbury K.G.*, 1886, vol. 2, p. 255.

I judged from his appearance that he had seen better days – his coat which was once Black was now Brown with age and worn thread bare, he had carefully button'd it up to his chin to hide what I afterward found to be his shirtless Body. his shoes were fresh clean'd but much the worse for wear – he was immaciated and care worn and altho a man in the prime of life there were evident marks of age in his shrivelled and writched countinance. He politely address'g me said. Pardon me Sir will you have the Kindness to by a few steel pins from me. I am Sir an old Drapers assistant out of employ and am doing this to keep me from starvation. I said I Know you are a Drapers assistant Mr. H. calling him by name at mention of which he litterally sprang from me recovering himself he said. do you Know me Sir? I replied I Knew you when you were a respectable man. Oh Sir when did you know me? at Cheltenham I said. at Scott's Sir? No I said I never Knew you at Scotts (I must here mention that Scott's was a celebrated public House in which Drapers assistants met after the Business of the day to smoke their pipe and drink in strong drinks each others health and happiness whilst in so doing they sacrificed their own) I lived with you I said at Messrs J (?) Ms' are you E.B. I am I said. Oh we look down upon you – true I said you were better educated – and a more experienced tradesman than myself and I never join'd you in your jovial Meeting I said – But Sir he said is this beautiful Shop yours – it is I replied oh what a contrast he said and the Big tear gather'd in his Eye – oh sir how did you get it. By saving the sixpences that you squander'd at Scotts I replied. But come in I said and having supplied in immediate wants I said tell your history and what brought you into the miserable condition. You may well say miserable Sir he said – but in a few words I will tell you – at Cheltenham I contracted the habit of drinking I was not fond of it but going night after night to spend a jovial hour I acquired the habit – I went to London and their I fill'd some excellent situations in two or three of the first class West End Drapery establishments – but drink – drink was my bane – However I married a respectable young woman, and went into business – I taught my wife to drink and in a little time she became as fond of drink as myself – we had many domestic broils. The gin palace was too frequently my resort and the resort too of my wife. One day we were both partly intoxicated – she had the Bottle in her hand to fetch some gin. We had words I much irritated her by what I said & while in a state of great excitement she took her scissors from her side and stabb'd herself to her heart and fell dead before my face. Oh sir he said what a scene was this and he burst into a flood of tears – Well sir since then I have been a Vagrant and outcast and wanderer upon the face of the earth – surely the wages of sin is death – I did what I could for his relief but found the habit of drunkenness and idleness so deeply rooted that no assistance from Man I fear will ever again reinstate him in his former happy and respectable condition –. . . .'[36]

There but for the Grace of God. . . .

Notes

1. Quoted in J. E. Hodder Williams, *The Life of Sir George Williams*, 1906, p. 36.
2. E. Hodder, *The Life of Samuel Morley*, 1887, p. 189.
3. Hodder, ibid., 199 et seq.
4. *Saturday Review*, 11 November 1905 (Selwyn Cuttings).
5. H. A. Walden, *Operation Textiles: A City Warehouse in Wartime*, n.d., (c. 1946), p. i.
6. Reproduced in *A New View of an Old House*, Souvenir Booklet published by Hitchcock, Williams and Co., n.d., (c. 1929), pp. 4–5.
7. The firm of Leaf, Hitchcock and Rogers; see *Weekly True Sun* Sunday, 30 April 1837 (typescript copy belonging to Hugh Williams Esq.); *Young Men's Christian Association, Occasional Paper No. 11 1855* (report of speeches at Opening of Aldersgate St. Y.M.C.A. 28 September 1854) p. 15.
8. Quoted in Alison Adburgham, *Shops and Shopping 1800–1914*, 1964, p. 279.
9. *9th Annual Report*, 1853–4, p. 17.
10. *Occasional Paper No. 11*, op. cit., pp. 15–16.
11. Hodder Williams, op. cit., pp. 47–63.
12. ibid., p. 51.
13. Alison Adburgham, op. cit., pp. 42–3.
14. Thus Charles Knight in 1851, quoted in Walden op. cit., p. vii and Alison Adburgham op. cit., p. 96.
15. ibid.
16. Alison Adburgham, op. cit., p. 143.
17. I am indebted to Miss L. M. Sieveking, the historian of Robert Sayle and Co., for this information.

18. *Diary* 10 October, 12 October 1894; *Lynn News* 11 November 1905 (Selwyn Cuttings); Pike's *Contemporary Biographies: Norfolk and Suffolk in the XXth Century*, Brighton 1911, p. 375.
19. Charles Knight in 1851, quoted in Alison Adburgham, op. cit., p. 97.
20. Hodder Williams, op. cit., p. 48; Alison Adburgham, op. cit., pp. 97–8.
21. Quoted in B. A. Yeaxlee, *Spiritual Values in Adult Education*, 2 vols., (O.U.P., 1925) vol. I, p. 170.
22. G. A. Sala in 1859, quoted in Alison Adburgham op. cit., p. 98. When did the euphemism 'in business' first become common among shop assistants?
23. ibid., p. 231.
24. *Schoolmaster*, 11 November 1905 (Selwyn Cuttings).
25. *3rd Annual Report*, 1847, pp. 10–11.
26. *18th Annual Report*, 1862–3, p. 11.
27. E. P. Hood, *Thomas Binney: His Mind, Life and Opinions*, 1874, p. 16.
28. *2nd Annual Report*, 1846, pp. 19–20.
29. J. C. Symons, *The History and Advantages of Young Men's Associations*, Melbourne (Australia) 1856, pp. 3–4.
30. W. E. Shipton, *The Young Men's Christian Association in London, its History, Objects and Development: A Report Presented to the Conference of Young Men's Christian Associations, Held in Paris, in August 1855*, p. 5.
31. E. Hodder, *The Life & Work of the 7th Earl of Shaftesbury K.G.*, 1886, 3 vols. vol. II, p. 523.
32. Hood, op. cit., p. 146.
33. 'Mark Rutherford', *The Revolution in Tanners Lane*, 1893, (10th imp. 1923) p. 145.
34. Hodder, *Shaftesbury*, op. cit., vol. II, p. 163.
35. ibid., p. 350.
36. MSS by Edward Beaumont, senior, Nat. Counc. MSS.

BOOK II

The Y.M.C.A. and its Setting

CHAPTER V

Two Diaries: George Williams and Edward Valantine in 1843 and 1844

There is a tradition which does not now seem to be verifiable, that George Williams entered the employment of Hitchcock, Rogers on 18 October 1841, that C. W. Smith who first suggested the name Young Men's Christian Association arrived in the same month, and that others of the founder members – Edward Valantine, Edward Beaumont, and William Creese among them – appeared in the course of the next two years.[1] There is a certainty, which goes beyond mere tradition, that in the course of the next three years an intense religious spirit was at work within the Hitchcock establishment. It was not unique to No. 72 St. Paul's Churchyard, except in the weeks leading up to June 1844 when the intensity became quite remarkable. It is also certain that no man contributed more to this atmosphere than George Williams, who was yet neither the most articulate nor the most far-sighted of his ardent companions. 'The strange thing is that the man who accomplished these things was of singularly limited interests, and really believed that young men can be satisfied with interests as limited as his own . . . All that he really cared for was, as he would put it, the saving of their souls . . . He was a wonderful instance of intense devotion to one purpose.'[2] This was typical of the sensible comments made by the secular press at the time of his death, yet the really strange thing is that anyone could describe the saving of souls as a 'singularly limited interest'.

The primary source for this period is the diaries kept by Williams and Valantine. Perhaps 'diaries' is misleading. It was not their concern to portray daily happenings in great detail. They fit instead into a recognizable category, the equivalent in their own limited way of W. E. Gladstone's private diaries. Their authors' prime concern was to describe their spiritual condition and other events were included only if they helped in this. They are desultory and hurried little volumes, the work of literate but under-educated, over-worked and over-anxious young men. They are remarkably alike, although Valantine's is slightly more revealing. Within these limits there nonetheless emerges a full account of an uncomfortable and repetitive existence, made tolerable by spiritual excitement. The books are full of questioning, but it is only religious questioning. There is no discontent, save at their spiritual inadequacy. They permitted themselves no imagination, save at the state of their souls. Two complementary personalities emerge. The young men were similar in age and social background. Edward Valantine was slightly older – he was 24 in May 1843; George Williams was better placed. Valantine came from the Midlands. He had worked in Nottingham, he had an ex-soldier brother in Sheffield, a dying father in Mansfield, and a sailor brother who was lost at sea. The material prospects of both families greatly outweighed their spiritual future, or so it seemed to their downcast draper sons. Like Williams, Valantine had been drawn to Congregationalism before coming to London, and in London he attended the Weigh House.

Both men were prone to religious introspection as their faith seemed to expect of them, but only Valantine was introspective by nature. Williams was worried lest he be too positive for a serious person; Valantine need have no such worries. There comes a warmth through the rather touching pieties of Williams's diaries. When he 'had a nice bit of chat with Brother Brown on Soul prosperity', it is the 'nice bit of chat' which is the operative phrase.[3] Williams loved his creature comforts in the midst of an uncomfortable life and his guilt at them was unavailing. His besetting sin of over-eating (and in November 1844 he promised 6d. to missions every time he over-indulged), his addiction to 'indolence and love of ease' shamed him.[4] There was an encouraging ordinariness about Williams, 'felt the want of being able to speak' (he was never a good public speaker in that age of oratory), 'gave way to temper with Rogers'.[5] There was a certainty about him which introspection failed to hide and which Valantine lacked.

Valantine too was tormented by 'unholy desires and sinful passions' ("I arose this a.m. with worldly thoughts originating from a dream") but there was a displeasing over-anxiousness about the old Adam in him: 'not been so Kind and obliging as I ought to have been in the shop', 'received a fresh supply of temporal blessings in the shape of money'.[6] He hoped 'to struggle more and more with my own sinful thoughts and feelings and bring my body into subjection' and he was 'Troubled in some measure by the wicked conversation of my Companions in my bedroom'.[7] Like Williams, Valantine was shy of uttering in public – the prospect of seconding a straightforward proposal about the division of funds at a meeting of the establishment's missionary auxiliary weighed heavily on him, although it was Williams's opinion that his friend made a 'few short pithy remarks much to the purpose'.[8] Unlike Williams he was no decision-maker and it was months before he could bring himself to *join* the Weigh House church though none would have doubted his fitness. There is a delightful atmosphere of dither about the marriage of Valantine's brother James to Christiana Feather. Edward did his best to take it all in hand and Christiana was fitted out at Hitchcock's. But 'James very nervous could scarcely write his name had an opportunity of praying with him', and afterwards the James Valantines missed their train at Euston and Edward lost a sovereign.[9]

There was something in the faith of both men at this time which brought out a negative streak in them. They felt keenly their spiritual estrangement from their families and their concern expressed itself in ways which make it easy to sympathize with their relatives. 'Wrote a long and I hope profitable letter to Bro. Robert on the requirements of the soul after conversion'.[10] 'Richard came up ... the Lord is blessing them temporally oh that his spirit may awaken them to a sense of sin'.[11] 'My relatives all that I know of going to Hell with the exception of an uncle what little effort have I made to save them', and there follows a prayer for his mother and the Robert Williamses and the William Williamses ('I believe they are the Lord's when his merciful time comes'), for the Johns, the Richards and Thomas and Charles ('These O Lord help me to plead with thee for until I prevail').[12]

Valantine found this sort of concern almost too much to bear when he was at his father's death-bed in August 1844. He was oppressed by the long hours of tedium involved in watching the sick-bed and he was appalled at his father's tone. Valantine tried to feel filial. He read the Bible, and gained no inspiration from it. He prayed aloud, and his father stopped him. 'Father's mind appeared rivetted to Earth ever rambling amongst scenes of business or pleasure'. Valantine asked if he were happy: 'I do not see why I should not be'. 'I asked him if he thought he should die, he said no he did not think he should, he did not appear to know the value of the Redeemer's blood.' Worst of all, at the well attended funeral, the fear, the certainty, that his father was not, could not be, in Heaven drove all other thoughts from him. No wonder he exasperated his mother.[13]

There is a deal of selfishness in personal religion and as yet neither Williams nor Valantine was free from it. It complicated Valantine's life in the shop and this entry appears amidst several suggesting bad feeling, '. . . a scene not altogether agreeable to myself my bed fellow Posnett (?) having slept out on a Sunday evening I reported him out, the next morning he was caught out by Mr. Hitchcock without leave and told him a falsehood was consequently dismissed'.[14] Understandably, Valantine was in great need of regular prayer with 'my friends', particularly George Williams whose maturity in spiritual matters was advancing, 'This evening was for the most part spent with George Williams had some happy moments of prayer this P.M. GW full of happiness the love of Christ being very precious.'[15]

There is one revealing thread running through the diaries – ill-health. Both Williams and Valantine were prone to the headaches, feverish colds and influenzas, and the sheer exhaustion which were the inevitable accompaniment to long hours, ill-ventilated accommodation and inadequate medical attention. Smallpox and sudden death harassed their colleagues making their own faith the more vital. They were lucky in that their worst, but by no means negligible, enemy was the weather, 'very cold and my heart just as cold as my hands'.[16]

Their attitude to their work is no less revealing. To Valantine, the dormitories at Hitchcock's were 'home'. To Williams they remained 'Hitchcock's'. Yet Valantine was less assured in his business than Williams, and his references to it were fewer. He arranged the linens for display in the shop in February 1843: in April he greeted the summer season with its extended hours; 'This week we begin to close at 9 p.m. and this leaves little time for devotion.'[17] Valantine was clearly well-regarded by his employer (he speaks on one occasion of 'my assistants', which suggests promotion)[18] yet when he was moved to the counting house ('a great change') it must have seemed that at last he had found his proper level.[19]

In contrast, George Williams was forthcoming in referring to his work. The numerous references suggest that despite occasional depressions he found his work to be well within his abilities. It engaged his interest: 'Had prosperous day in business', 'had a good day of Business – a pretty comfortable day', outnumbering 'rather dull in business'.[20] At times he is more explicit: 'extended carpet stock book a very difficult task' – he occasionally acted as a buyer. Like Valantine, he helped with window-dressing and had a 'pretty good' day with muslins and linens or later 'in the Cashmeres', or later still, 'Great Linen Show'. Williams was concerned at a business slump and noted surprisingly, 'Business so dull went out for a walk'.[21] One entry uncovers the rough justice which they took for granted, 'Glasson broke a large pane of glass cost 10£ young men subscribed nearly 3£'.[22]

Twice, although not without apology, Williams's enthusiasm broke through. In August 1843 he holidayed with his people visiting all the Williamses ('I have nearly a 100 Relatives'.), enquiring into their spiritual prosperity ('and only Uncle Norman sister H. K. Williams My Dear Mother Mrs. Thomas Williams Dulverton' were saved[23]) and immersing himself again in the spiritual and secular life of a farming community. On Friday, 18 August he went to an auction. It was crowded. Williams disliked the atmosphere and the auctioneer's patter irritated him. That evening he sought to raise the matter with the fellow, but found him 'far gone in drink': 'Oh the curse of being too anxious for money may even after such sins God be pleased to pass by the hardness of Robert's heart and grant him repentance unto life –' . . . and yet, as sales went, it was a good one.

About a year later in July 1844, a significant thing happened. Williams had his first experience of real advance in his trade. Much later J. C. Symons, with William Creese the Y.M.C.A.'s first secretary, irritated at the repeated statements that the movement was founded by an apprentice, would point out that Williams by 1844 'was the most important man in the house and buyer and manager of one of the largest departments'.[24] The direct evidence for this comes after the founding of the association, but it fits in with the picture of the young man who had reputedly turned down the opportunity to set up on his own account at Bridgwater. 'Mr. May discharged and Mr. H. asks me or rather offered for my consideration the drapery department as buyer.' Of course, Williams took it to the Lord in prayer, 'I ask not honour nor wealth nor the luxuries of this life, but to glorify thy name.' In his diary he wrote out a list of helpful texts and enumerated the points to be made for and against the post. He noted drawbacks like 'ungodly conversation' or 'much leisure time' but the advantages are truly revealing, 'manlike decision, judgement, taste. Knowledge of the Stock, Serving Wholesale Customers. Marking off Goods. Treatment of young men'. He did his best to make a difficult decision where surely there was none to make. 'Went to Mr. Meeking's for reference of Mr. Vernon had a bit of chat – Mr. Hitchcock very pleasant but not yet decided as to my filling Mr. Mays situation.' Surely God willed him to be thus promoted? 'Went to Harts Coffee House with Valantine and Brethren nice evening only eat a little too much have the hearty cooperation of all the brethren in the house'. Next day, 18 July, he was appointed, '. . . this day is a day of worldy [sic] exaltation', and he prayed for wisdom.

Work began at once amidst many good wishes. 'For the first time went into the market bought my first parcel at Sheriff and Co find I require much wisdom and judgment may the Lord bless and feed me.' He entered into it zestfully: 'bought Cobden's new prints' is a pleasant reminder of the Anti-Corn Law Leaguer's business concerns and a reminder too that Cobden's London warehouse was among the more tolerable for clerks and apprentices. For the three years before 1843 one of its clerks, William Holman Hunt, had occasionally designed ornamental cloths for display as samples to buyers from City business houses. A complaisant manager permitted the youth to cut a twelve hour working day to eight hours – the rest Hunt spent in museums and galleries.[25] I. and R. Morley's was among the warehouses which Williams visited early in August. It was already time to buy 'our winter stock of Welsh Flannels'.[26]

There was seldom time for recreation or more than a superficial cultivation of the intellect. Indeed, beyond the occasional outing such things were not proper to the drapers' station. Their refreshment in every sense was to be found in prayer meetings. It was only when relatives came to town that excursions to the Adelaide Gallery and the Polytechnic Institution could be fitted in. The Polytechnic played an important part in the lives of young Victorian Londoners and later in the century, transformed and extended by philanthropists, it complemented the activities of the London Y.M.C.A. Opened in 1838 in Regent Street, the Polytechnic was intended for scientific exhibitions. In the 1840s no country-man cared to omit it from his itinerary, least of all the experience of descending, at the cost of ear-ache, in its diving bell.[27]

Late in December 1843 brother Charles Williams was marched round the General Post Office, the Bank, the Tower, the House of Lords, Westminster Abbey, 'Mdam Tushawes' and the Chinese Exhibition – which Valantine was only able to see a little later in January, in an unsuccessful attempt to shake off 'flu.[28] Such jaunts were dangerous. In July 1844 Valantine toured 'the cartoons Westminster Hall castings etc', taking in the Abbey, the National Gallery and the Adelaide Gallery, 'very much pleased but found that these visits tend much to deaden the spiritual life in the soul'.[29] Mercifully these artistic jaunts were exceptional, to be inflicted on country mice. For themselves there was a rare state occasion – the Queen and the Prince returning from opening Parliament looking very well, or the Queen opening the Royal Exchange, in October 1844. That was a particularly delicious time because Hitchcock's had a whole holiday which enabled Valantine to accompany Mr. Fearon and a party of young ladies to Greenwich Park. They spent a 'very spiritual and happy day'.[30]

More often there was the undemanding relaxation of the Holborn Baths 'our conversation there being upon the goodness of God in the provision of his mercies to man', or a pleasant half-hour at a Temperance Coffee House.[31] As a culmination of joy, because a fair measure of usefulness was involved, there was the sort of social meeting which Victorians developed to a fine art. One in particular is noted in the diaries. On Good Friday 1843, five of the brethren travelled south to Brixton and the greenery of Tulse Hill and Norwood Cemetery. Valantine dutifully noted the 'fruit trees richly laden with blossoms' and Williams professed himself 'very much delighted' with the 'putting forth of Spring' and the 'fresh air and grandeur of scenery'. They returned from the grandeur of Norwood Cemetery via the Thames Tunnel, where the crowds prevented their admittance, and so ended with Pentonville's annual Good Friday Teetotal Tea. The speakers, who included a 'Scotch Baronet', were men of substance – a point not to escape Williams – and the speeches were, so Valantine felt, 'most beautiful and very convincing'. So convincing that Valantine, to Williams's delight, signed the pledge believing it 'to be an act of Divine providence thus to make teetotalism an instrument in bringing many out of nature's darkness to the knowledge of the truth'. Williams found it all 'a time ever to be remembered'.

Williams appended, incoherently and unsatisfactorily (he cannot really have understood the speaker to have identified 'The antient

Brittons' with Puritans) his notes of the main speech by Mr. Buckingham. James Silk Buckingham had been a noted Radical M.P. in the
1830s and he was, like many Radicals, crotchety and capricious in his
enthusiasms. He had become widely-known as a lecturer for temperance causes and in 1843 he had returned from a visit to the
United States. It is intriguing to find in Williams's impressions
of what Buckingham had said, the traditional Radical dislike
of unnecessary public expenditure asserting that demon drink
caused expensive workhouses, expensive lunatic asylums, expensive
prisons and police stations, and the expensive transportation of
convicts.[32]

Teetotalism in the 1840s was the sort of crotchet likely to appeal
to Radicals, and the few political allusions which the diaries contain
reflect very much the liberal world of the Weigh House. Sir Robert
Peel and the high politicians of Westminster are nowhere named,
and Cobden only appears by virtue of his calicoes, but the ripples
caused by England's first modern administration reached St. Paul's
Churchyard even though they created little enthusiasm – 'A great
Anti Corn Law Ligue [*sic*] Meeting Drury Lane Theatre was invited
to attend as steward but declined'.[33] What did arouse concern,
because it was an issue most likely to move Binney in the pisgah of
his pulpit, was the problem of Church and State and its effect on
education. In the 1840s this was reaching a new bitterness, complicating traditional politics and ecumenical effort in an unprecedented
way. The Maynooth Grant, the Disruption of the Church of Scotland,
the formation of the Anti-State Church Association and the educational clauses which were tacked on to Sir James Graham's Factory
Bill, all events of the years 1843 to 1845, aroused a general interest
in interrelated political, religious and educational matters which was
to be maintained for much of the century.

London Nonconformity was especially stirred by such controversies. The bitterness which was aroused forced the capital's Dissenters to a prominence which allowed little compromise. This was of
the greatest importance in the pre-history of the 'Nonconformist
Conscience'. It was of hardly less significance in delaying and altering
the development of united Christian action. Nowhere were the
implications of this clearer than in the life of Andrew Reed who
organized Dissenting opposition to Graham's bill.

By 1840 Reed was admired and famous in the world of philanthropy. His orphan asylum at Clapton was up-to-date and successful,

and his infant asylum at Wanstead was assured of prosperity, when on 24 June 1841, in brilliant weather and surrounded by 'an array of goodness and beauty', the Prince Consort laid the memorial stone.[34] Reed had scaled the summits of philanthropic endeavour. The Queen, the Prince and the Queen Dowager were patrons of his schemes, Mr. Byng and Lords Howe and Duncannon were at hand if bureaucracy had to be circumvented, the Duke of Wellington could be prevailed upon to preside at dinners for the charities. A Dissenting parson could not ask for more.

At this point sectarianism supervened. Disputes arose over the catechism to be used in the Wanstead asylum. By 1843 the board of governors was divided over the matter and Reed, who objected both to the use of a catechism for infants and of a Church catechism when there was no alternative asylum to cater for Dissenters, was in the minority. On 23 February 1843 he resigned all connexion with Wanstead and feeling unable to attend the grand opening by the King of the Belgians he wandered disconsolately in the neighbouring woods 'like a silly bird fluttering about the nest from which some rude hand had driven it. This is the martyrdom of the nineteenth century'.[35] He turned to the provision of a non-denominational orphanage and the new venture was attended with the usual success but it involved another painful wrench. Reed, whose life had been spent in philanthropic diplomacy, now considered that he could not consistently maintain his connexion with the London Orphan Asylum at Clapton, the first of his charities. On Thursday, 6 June 1844 he told a deputation that his decision was irrevocable, he must break the tie which had lasted for thirty years. The issues were sectarian, and as for Christian unity, 'I am myself a living instance of its impracticability at present'.[36]

So far the tragedy was a personal one for Reed. Its implications, however, were appreciated by London Dissenters and Reed's supporters for the new, unsectarian asylum included James Nisbet the publisher (and later a supporter of the Y.M.C.A.), James Sherman of the Surrey Chapel, and Alderman Wire, a self-made businessman who, with his brother, was prominent at the Weigh House. But surrounding these events was the national controversy about education which crystallized so many religious jealousies.

Reed's concern for education had grown since his interest in Brougham's schemes of 1816. Early in 1843, Sir James Graham introduced his much-needed Factory Bill. It contained educational clauses which, if accepted, would have gone far towards providing some form of national education. But the clauses were phrased with a marvellous disregard for Dissenting susceptibilities. Dissent of all kinds was strong in factory districts; the Bill was weighted in favour of the National Church. 'My attention,' Reed later recalled, 'was awakened by reading Sir James Graham's speech. . . . It was plausible and sentimental, and meant to conciliate all parties. But it seemed to me, in fact, to be prepared to strike a deadly blow at our liberties.'[37]

Reed took prompt action. On 8 March, a fortnight after he had resigned from the Wanstead asylum, the first of a series of sectional meetings was held in London. Sympathetic M.P.s were mobilized, a manifesto was drawn up, and a central committee was organized. Reed overcame the daintiness of his fellow ministers – he scoured London and then toured sixteen counties to organize an apparently spontaneous agitation. Baptists, Quakers, and Wesleyans were drawn in and petitions were presented in their hundreds at the House of Commons. The abilities which had organized philanthropy were admirably suited to political activity, and there could be little doubt about the political impact of the matter when Reed delivered his conscience before an embarrassed Lord John Russell at the British School Society's Annual Meetings in the Exeter Hall. 'We ask, in short, that we shall be free: in labour, free; in trade, free; in action, free; in thought, free; in speech, free; in religion, free – perfectly free. We ask freedom for others, freedom for ourselves, freedom for all, without distinction, that breathe in British air, and rest on British soil . . . for where is the Englishman that would wish to survive his liberties?'[38] The bill was withdrawn in the summer of 1843.

The Reed family continued to be identified with philanthropy, but their dangerous association with political Dissent was scarcely less apparent. Yet if passions had been aroused, so had the potential of London's young men. The donkey work in the agitation had been undertaken by a committee of young men, formed in the vestry of Reed's Wycliffe Chapel, off the Commercial Road. It met daily at seven in the morning, breakfast concluding each two-hour session and it met again each night. The secretary was Reed's younger son Charles at that time in his early twenties and engaged to the youngest daughter of Edward Baines, whose *Leeds Mercury* co-ordinated the campaign in the provinces. Since 1842, Charles Reed had been in business as a printer at Bolt Court, Fleet Street, and he was building up a useful and potentially powerful Dissenting connexion. The work of his committee culminated on 2 June 1843, when a petition was presented signed by 25,000 Young Men of London.[39]

It was here that the national agitation impinged upon Mr. Hitchcock's young men, for at the Weigh House on the Easter Sunday after the Pentonville Teetotal Tea, Valantine listened to Binney inveighing against the Graham proposals. Three weeks before this the Weigh House teachers had signed a 'partition' against the proposals, one of the 13,350 which had been presented by 9 May.[40] Charles Reed's committee and his organizing abilities had other results because flushed with victory, Andrew Reed, with his son in the background, acted with Edward Baines, Samuel Morley and other leading Dissenters in the negotiations leading to a Congregational Board of Education. Its secretary, Robert Ainslie, was personally known at Hitchcock's.[41] Such was the atmosphere surrounding the likeliest sources of Dissenting support for a Y.M.C.A., and the undercurrents likely to complicate its existence.

As yet, however, the problems of Church and State were at some remove from George Williams. He knew little of the Church of England and he rather disliked what he saw. It displeased him at the Percy Chapel that 'a Mr. Wood preached without a bible' and his only reference to St. Paul's, whose shadow could scarcely be ignored by any young man at No. 72, was uncomplimentary. Williams and Valantine went there on the occasion of the Festival of the Sons of the Clergy. Valantine enjoyed the 'beautiful singing', but Williams wrote shortly, 'the singing good but the other part an empty show of pomp'.[42] It is not surprising that he later overheard a long discussion on the Establishment, 'its evils as well as its good' or that, on holiday in Somerset, he 'had a long chat on Church and State Baptismal regeneration and other important points could not agree'.[43]

The well-engineered popular uproar which Graham's proposals caused was in part a reflection of the widespread enthusiasm for mutual improvement. The diaries are not solely concerned with spiritual matters varied occasionally with a jaunt and tempered delicately with politics. Indeed, in view of the Y.M.C.A.'s later preoccupation with the place in it of education, it is interesting to find in the diaries an awareness of the mind accompanying a growth in religious intensity. It was a separate growth, altogether on a lower key, but it was distinctive. Perhaps it reflected naturally the need for assistants in a fashionable business to better themselves for their own success. Drapers must be presentable and must gauge precisely what is acceptable. A 'little too much pride existing in my heart with respect to dress', Valantine noted in July 1844.[44]

George Williams was always a dapper little man. He was also, like most middle-class men, an uncertainly educated man. There was a breathlessness about his grammar. His spelling was poor and it remained so – this very fact demonstrates his need for self-improvement. 'Spent part of the day with Bro John who came to Town for the first time went to the Polaticnic Instition and Madam Dusors eveng, heard no very favourable account of the spiritual progress at home.'[45] Polaticnic Instition and Madam Dusors? If he spelt words as he heard them or was learning to pronounce them, it is not over-fanciful to detect the clipped deferential accent of the good shopman replacing what remained of 'Somersetshire'. Provincial accents were tolerated remarkably late in aristocratic circles. Middle-class provincials with their way to make in London could not afford such luxuries. 'Join'd the elocution recited a Piece by Byron hope it will be the means of doing me some good', he noted in November 1843. A week later Valantine returned to Hitchcock's in time for part of Mr. Thornton's lecture on elocution. 'Mr. Branch* was with us and enlivened the meeting much'.[46]

Williams's first excursion into things of the mind concerned music (he insisted on calling it Mussa or Mussae or Mussac). The great age of popular music was beginning. Tonic-Sol-fa, the most successful popularizer of vocal music and to all intents the invention of John Curwen, a young Congregational minister and friend of Charles Reed, was in its infancy. In 1843, Curwen published his *Grammar of Vocal Music*. His method was an attractive one and there was something immensely moral about it all. The Weigh House was quick to utilize this aid to family music. At the Exeter Hall another system, no less welcome in Evangelical circles, was in vogue. From February 1841 John Hullah ran a series of classes to train day and Sunday school teachers in vocal music. Far more than teachers attended Hullah's school and in educational circles he was the centre of controversy and admiration. In 1844 he became Professor of Vocal Music at King's College in the Strand.[47]

Hitchcock's young men were not immune from the contagion of such musical experiment. On Friday, 13 January 1843, copying others in the house, Williams, Valantine and three more went 'to learn

* See Chapter VI, p. 113.

singing for the first time at Exeter Hall'. The day had been a very windy one and Valentine was battling with a cold as well as stock-taking. Despite this he and Williams were pleased by it. For some months they soldiered on, Valentine rather more happily than Williams. They practised regularly, 'learnt the Diatonic major scale', 'commenced beating time', 'practised singing in 9 bed with 5 others. How great is the goodness and longsuffering of God'. Inevitably there was the self-warning: 'The mind rather cold and barren after thinking of our mussac lesson'. For Valentine the practice of singing before breakfast tended to worldly thoughts.[48]

For Williams it was a passing phase, but one worthy of note if only because the lessons were held in the Exeter Hall. That building represented for him all that was best in the outside world. For fifty years of the nineteenth century it was the centre of Evangelical England, the very portals of Orthodoxy. For twenty years more it was the headquarters of the London Y.M.C.A. It was also, until the building of the Royal Albert Hall, the centre of London's musical world. The three causes intermingle. It was at the Exeter Hall that the pious middle-classes could listen, at first suspiciously, to sacred oratorios and then because the surroundings were so blameless, learn to accept them and even to participate in them. It was also at the Exeter Hall that the great May Meetings of the Nonconformist sects, the Missionary Societies, and all the triumphant paraphernalia of Evangelicalism were held. Briefly, in that religious month of May, 'the Church and Conventicle meet together, the Platform and the Pulpit kiss each other',[49] although in an increasingly political age such vocal unity was bound to be a prelude to less polite activity elsewhere. It was when the building was in danger of becoming an inferior music hall that the Y.M.C.A. was able to save some at least of its grander associations.

When Williams first knew it, it was a modern building (completed in 1831) facing the Strand massively, narrowly, and a shade blindly. In addition to its office space it contained three halls of which the largest held 3,000. As with all such buildings, its acoustics were criticized and its ventilation was dubious, but it was much loved by good men.

The Tuesday evenings spent there appeared prominently in the diaries before being replaced by more solid fare. Neither Williams nor Valentine was devoted to books beyond the one Book. In February 1843 Williams read 'a little of Decapolis by Mr. Ford of

Leamington'.* It took him rather over a week. A year later Valantine took advantage of a sore throat to spend a day in the establishment's library reading 'Edmondson's *Self Govt.*'† There are few other such references but Williams's entry about 'Decapolis' is interesting. It was part of a full, if spiritually depressing, day in which he 'got past the lark' in 'Mussac', and dressed windows in business. He also noted, 'Brown and Smith commenced giving short lectures in No 2 bedroom.'

It is probable that these short lectures were not entirely on religious topics and that they belong to the pre-history of the establishment's Mutual Improvement Society. In view of the later concern of Y.M.C.A. leaders to stress the wholly spiritual nature of their first meetings it is important to note that the prayer meetings which prepared the way for the Association were accompanied at Hitchcock's by more secular meetings which were separately organized but nonetheless initiated and dominated by the same young men and the same principles. On 4 November 1843 Valantine was elected to the committee of the newly formed society. Williams noted, 'a meeting in No 1 as to the best way of conducting the winters lectures for the profit of all – a long debate'.[50] Thereafter its activities displaced music.

The meetings were a mixture. Some were conducted by more intellectually gifted brethren – C. W. Smith on the Hebrew Scriptures 'and a beautiful lecture it was' or later on Astronomy 'illustrated by transparencies' and giving 'general satisfaction'.[51] There was a firmly religious bias and Mr. Ablett's 'Fulfillment of Profecy' and Mr. Symmons (i.e. J. C. Symons) on the persecution of the early Christian Church were typical, but there was also a most respectable collection of outside speakers.[52] The 'Mr. Ainsley', for example, who gave the inaugural lecture on the history of the Jews in England (a 'delightful' evening) was the Revd. Robert Ainslie, at that time a Congregational minister. Ainslie had been associated with the London City Mission since its inception in 1835, and from 1839 to 1844 he acted as one of its secretaries. Then, when the educational controversies aroused his

* This was David Everard Ford, *Decapolis: or, the Individual Obligations of Christians to Save Souls from Death. An Essay*, 1840. Williams's *Diary*, 25 February 1843.

† This was Jonathan Edmondson, *A Concise System of Self Government in the great affairs of Life and Godliness on Scriptural and Rational Principles*, 1816. Valantine's *Diary*, 7 February 1844.

denomination, he became first secretary to the Congregational Board of Education. Ainslie was a not undistinguished scholar whose learning led him far from accepted orthodoxy.[53] A little later Dr. Leifchild's literary son gave a course of lectures on Geology ('very interesting') and on Coal Mines and Mining ('very instructive'). If these lectures were the core of what he later produced in book form they must have been fascinating as well as instructive because the younger John Leifchild was an accomplished popularizer.[54] Dr. Scott, alas, on Mental Culture, was 'very interesting but not delivered in the way expected'.[55]

It was perhaps impossible for these activities to be viewed in any other light than their likely religious usefulness. But they did prove useful. They also proved that the house's religious young men were also the house's most generally alert young men, a lesson which the Y.M.C.A. endeavoured to teach whomsoever would listen. Yet they were only means to a grander end.

Enough is known of the religious atmosphere which surrounded Williams and his friends to place them firmly in the Evangelical world. Yet even here, as elsewhere in Williams's life, the certainty is only apparent. He was without doubt an Evangelical. Hodder Williams felt that to the end he clung almost fiercely to the doctrines of the guilt of man and the wrath of God and his family were under no illusions as to their father's beliefs.[56] George Williams was not a naturally introspective man and not too much should be read into the glooms and despondencies of parts of his diary. Neither was he unthoughtful, and while an attached congregation could sit happily under a beloved pastor listening to doctrines they would not tolerate elsewhere, there was surely sufficient conflict between Finney's Perfectionism and Binney's embattled optimism, let alone Leifchild's hell-surrounded heavens, to have provoked thought. Yet the diaries are passive on this matter. Williams and Valantine examine themselves, they commit all things to God, they are meticulous in their attendance at worship, at prayer meetings, at teachers' meetings and at missionary meetings. While despondency abounds in their diaries, there is no real doubt – there is not even questioning.

George Williams was already a committed church member when he arrived in London. Valantine was not. While in business in Nottingham he sat under Richard Alliott, a well known Congregationalist of the time, and when Alliott removed to York Road Chapel, Lambeth, Valantine dutifully and sentimentally attended his ministry.

Yet he still felt unworthy of membership.[57] In January 1843 Valantine was reading John Angell James's *Anxious Enquirer* and he regarded Angell James as his 'father in Christ'.[58] In March he attended the Weigh House ordinance with his friend Williams, 'I remained a spectator and O how my spirit wished to join the Church and to fulfil the commandment of our blessed Lord.'[59] Two days later Valantine read a pamphlet on the Lord's Supper. It had been a frustrating day, 'was tried by sinful men they causing the law of sin to rise in the shape of ill feeling'.[60] It was a difficult time for him. By the end of March, Valantine determined to see Binney about joining the church, yet in May he still yearned for the day when he might sit with the fellowship and share the sacrament with them.[61] It was not until 15 October, after much praying about it, that Valantine actually consulted his dear pastor: 'oh may its events never be obliterated from my mind'.[62] A month later he was interviewed by one of the deacons ('Oh Lord teach me to live that I may adorn this important office') and on 2 January 1844, after yet another delay, Valantine wrote, 'This the most eventful day I ever saw is come and nearly past.'

It began pleasantly: 'enjoyed some happy thoughts while dressing the window'. Mr. Hitchcock went out of his way to be helpful. 'After tea G. Williams and I left the shop to prepare for chapel', and there follows an account of what happened there. They sang a hymn, a deacon prayed and Binney twice addressed the twelve candidates for membership. The first time Binney spoke practically and with great sympathy, the second time he touched upon doctrinal matters and he dealt with the Communion service, that it might bring 'before our hearts the subject of the great sacrifice our Lords death that holy thoughts and purposes should be kindled and thus our love increased and spiritual strength renewed'. Seen through the eyes of Edward Valantine it still appears as a moving service despite the changes of fashion and expression in the intervening century. It is pleasant to find this echoed by Williams, Valantine's fellow-member and worker who had watched anxiously over his friend, 'Went with Mr. Valantine who was admitted as a member to the Weigh Hs church. Mr. Binney gave them a suitable address may the Lord enable him to hold on his way.' It was, as Binney pointed out to them, so important that 1844, the new year, should begin well.[63]

For all the persistent soul-searching this is the closest that either of the diaries comes to religious *intimacy* and even here there is no inkling of private beliefs. Elsewhere there is an occasional gleam, 'How good is God in not sending me to Hell' is a comment of unexpected assurance for Williams. Only a converted and a Calvinist man could have made it.[64] There is the occasional disparagement of 'Pusism and error' and one unexpected entry reveals a conflict of emotion, 'Xmas day. Went morng to Roman Catholic Chapel very much disgusted Oh that God would have mercy upon such opposition to His simple truth.' Only a saved Calvinist could have felt such doubt about God's loving kindness, but then the whole excursion had been caused by the annoying fact of the Finsbury Chapel being over-crowded.[65] There is, interestingly enough, only one reference (and that by Valantine) to revivalism. In July 1844, Valantine stayed with his brother Fred in Sheffield. Amidst family prayers and hymns with the neighbours he spent Sunday morning at Brunswick Methodist Chapel, 'Spent a nice day heard Mr. Cowen the great N.Y. or American revivalist . . . very impressive Chapel crowded to excess sat in the childrens gallery.' In the evening he listened to Mr. Muir, the pastor of Queen Street Congregational Church who followed up the campaign with a 'very arousing sermon intended to awaken the sinner and lead him to Christ Jesus'.*

There remains in this connexion a further disappointing aspect of the diaries. They list the ministers heard and the texts expounded, but where notes are appended they contain little that is truly note-worthy, beyond the Evangelical commonplaces of the day. Yet the pastors they heard were not commonplace and their sermons were more than 'beautiful' which was Valantine's usual description of them. One wishes to know more of the effect of Binney's 'funeral sermon to young men – on the death of a young woman' or the sermon 'from which . . . it remained on our minds our duty when married'.[66] Binney's funeral sermon for John Clayton, his respectable predecessor, is known to have contained moving and perceptive passages.[67] Only once is there a glimpse of the real Binney. As Valantine recorded it in his garbled way, 'though man may appear outwardly to walk in a calm and undisturbed way having his mind seared as it were with a hot iron, yet he may be the subject of inward or private transgressions against God which if not repented of will form those combustible materials which in the day of death will

---

* Valantine's *Diary*, 22 July 1844. 'Mr. Cowen' was in fact James Caughey who conducted a revivalist campaign in Sheffield Methodist chapels for some months in 1844. I am indebted to Mr. R. J. Carwardine for this information.

light up a flame within the soul which will burn everlastingly'.[68] This is a far cry from everlasting torments, although the words are burning ones.

'. . . How swift the time is passing on and ere long thou will leave all that is near and dear to thee on earth make good use of thy time as Whitefield did in bringing souls to Christ'.[69] Their faith was worthless unless reflected in missionary work. It was missionary aggressiveness as much as intensity of devotion which characterized the Y.M.C.A. and the lives of its founders, and which informs their surviving diaries. Williams had served a missionary apprenticeship at Bridgwater, and in London his time was over-full with Sunday and Ragged School work, with open-air preaching and the promotion of missionary endeavour. Valantine was no less enthusiastic.

School work occupies most space of this sort in the diaries. Sunday School work naturally led Williams and some of his associates into the Ragged School movement which was expanding at this time and beginning to draw Lord Ashley's attention to the gutters of the metropolis. The progression was natural because not even the most reputable of Victorian Sunday Schools could be called respectable. Church members seldom considered it desirable to send their own children to Sunday School. The Sunday School, in the south especially, was for the poor – preferably the good poor, often the very poor. The teachers were untrained and their help was usually voluntary. Too often they were not themselves church members. Their work was always unpleasant and sometimes dangerous. To persevere in it and enjoy it suggest an almost invulnerable toughness. Later stories of Williams accosting every ship's hand while crossing the Atlantic and discussing their soul welfare, or embarrassing his sons by expecting them to be as importunate as he in tract distribution, fall more easily into place when his period at Darby Street or Jurston Street is recalled. It is significant that Williams's diary gives no inkling of the difficulties involved, for these one must turn to Edward Valantine – 'the boys rather more still and I enjoyed the situation', 'Williams and I out with the boys who were troublesome', 'boys inattentive', 'one of my boys very unruly', 'very wet, boys refractory, little good done', all these were the hazards of the Weigh House Schools. Those of Darby Street and Jurston Street were far greater.[70]

Darby Street was the headquarters of what became the Weigh House Domestic Mission. It had grown from the activities of the church's Christian Instruction Society, similar to that at Craven

Chapel, which had been founded in 1831. From 1842 the manifold activities of this society concentrated upon hired premises in Darby Street which, in the course of the 1840s, became a mission in its own right with its own committee and trustees. The church took the mission seriously. Samuel Morley was chairman of the trustees, in 1846 Ebenezer Pye Smith became treasurer of the mission, and sub-scribers and workers in the 1850s included his former pupil Samuel Habershon, Matthew Hodder, Jeremiah and Edward Colman, and Andrew Reed's associate, Alderman Wire.[71] George Williams was involved in Sunday work there at least from 1843, comprising school in the morning and afternoon, and a service in the evening. It was the week-day work which developed into a Ragged School.[72]

In January 1843, Williams became secretary to the Chapel Sunday School itself, 'may not this office rise my vanity.'[73] Thereafter his Sundays were devoted to the schools. Valantine followed in the wake of his friend and for him the step involved the usual heart-searching and dither. He attended teachers' prayer meetings ('I was called upon and did engage, it being the first time in publick'), he helped with some teaching – but it was some time before he actually became a full teacher and took his turn sitting in the gallery with the children, with George Williams comfortingly there beside him on this trying occasion.[74] And it was later still that Valantine went to help at Darby Street ('to oblige my friend Williams'), speaking to the children on God is Love – 'they were rather restless I manag'd very well some of them paying great attention'.[75]

From January 1844 Williams's concerns widened. He took in another school in an equally difficult area, this time south of the river at Jurston Street, Southwark. There was a double significance in this, for it brought him further into the Ragged School movement (and the Ragged School Union was formed in this year, with R. C. L. Bevan, the banker and future patron of the Y.M.C.A., as treasurer) and it linked him with London's best-known Sunday Schools, those connected with the Surrey Chapel.

The Jurston Street School had been founded in 1816 although it had been in Jurston Street only since 1835 when new purpose-built premises had been opened. Four years later, in 1839, an evening Ragged School was opened there, and by 1845 Jurston Street had 315 children and 48 teachers on its books, with 230 children and 78 teachers on the books of its Ragged School. Jurston Street was surrounded by the greyest poverty and teaching there was difficult even by London standards. Walter Williams, one of the founders, was said to have been nearly blinded by a missile hurled by a pupil. In 1841 the school's report described the Ragged School 'whose scholars are of the poorest and most depraved character, have scarcely any clothes to cover them, are destitute of the first elements of knowledge, and seem unaccustomed to any kind of subordination save that of force'. Neither were the scholars little boys – they were young men in their late 'teens 'exceedingly disorderly and riotous'.[76] Williams and Valantine faced them, Valantine as usual noting the problems, 'lads made a great noise by turning up sparrows in the school'.[77] On one occasion a merciful Providence delayed him, 'was obliged to stay behind in consequence of medicine operating freely'.[78]

But the teachers at Jurston Street were not entirely on their own. They were part of the many-branched and carefully organized South-wark Sunday School Society, a group of schools and missions nurtured by the Surrey Chapel. In the year ending February 1845 the Society taught 4,441 children and it had 546 teachers. The teachers had to undergo a period of probation before they were fully accepted, and the activities of devoted superintendents, great functions such as the annual New Year Teachers' Tea, and over all the commanding figure of James Sherman, the Surrey Chapel's pastor, provided an atmosphere of efficiency and enthusiasm which was almost unique.[79] The schools were able to build on the experience of fifty years. Surrey Chapel itself claimed to have had a Sunday School since 1786 but the School Society had been founded in the autumn of 1799.[80] The inspiration for this had come from Thomas Cranfield, a journeyman tailor whose early life was indeed filled with the excess which pious books liked to attribute to the unconverted. The whole of his life was passed on the borders of poverty and it was complicated by the fluctuations of a nervous and disorganized temperament. Despite this the schools which Cranfield had founded in 'the very heart of Satan's dominions' survived well into the twentieth century, a striking testimony to his inspiration and the tenacity of his successors.[81] They had pioneered a Sweeps' Sunday School in 1817, the Jurston Ragged School in 1839, and they showed a particular awareness of the needs of young people between the ages of 15 and 25, 'a period of life more important and perilous than any other. Comparatively few conversions take place after that age ... [While] temptations ... to yield to the lusts and passions of depraved nature, are unusually strong'.[82]

The importance of all this for Williams and Valantine cannot be overstressed. The Sunday School provided ardent young men with a first, sometimes terrifying, lesson in articulateness. When Andrew Reed was first asked to pray at Ponders End, 'I was so overwhelmed that I kept away for some weeks'.[83] It faced them with the need to expound doctrine in the simplest terms – Reed's first address had been from Isaiah xxxiii.[14] 'Fearfulness hath surprised the hypocrites'.[84] Thomas Cranfield shirked no horrors:

'One day, after energetically urging his youthful hearers to flee from the wrath to come, he exclaimed, "children, do you know whither you are going? Did you ever in your life, for a moment, think, whether you are going to heaven or hell? If not, think of it now. Do not delay: time is precious, and the next moment may hurry you into an eternal world. Oh! do examine yourselves: let each one ask himself, and herself, Am I going to heaven or hell?" and then taking out his watch, he laid it on the desk, and said, "Come, I will give you three minutes to think of the matter." The children, during this time, remained in the most profound silence; and there is no doubt, that many seriously considered the question.'[85]

For Charles Reed, who devoted much of his life to the cause, the early Sunday Schools were for most 'the chief means of intellectual and of religious progress', and he believed that their influence was very much responsible for 'the law-abiding spirit of our people'.[86] It was possible, when considering the Surrey Chapel Schools, to entertain such hopes. From January 1844, Williams's Sundays comprised Darby Street in the morning, the Weigh House Schools in the afternoon, and Jurston Street in the evening. The aspirations which these aroused were easily transferred to the different circumstances of a Y.M.C.A. Inevitably, the Weigh House Sermons fade into the background, although the figure of Binney regularly and affectionately addressing his Sunday School Children, urging even them to manly self-improvement, remains powerfully attractive.

The Victorians were capable of incredible industry. It is possible when considering Williams's later involvement with the Y.M.C.A. and his every breath devoted to its welfare, to explain this by arguing that his prosperity permitted servants, an easily-run household, and an efficiently-handled business. In the 1840s, Williams had none of these advantages and he still fitted in enough philanthropy for a dozen men. It was not enough that he teach for the Weigh House and the Surrey Chapel, he must probe further and work for Craven Chapel too. And Valantine and the brethren must work with him. His friendship with Craven's Mr. Cutting ripened. It introduced Williams to clever young men from the theological colleges at Homerton and Highbury, and once he dined at Homerton. It also introduced him to house-to-house visiting of an aggressive kind, 'visited the cottages around Paddington Green and preached the Gospel to the poor in their dwellings', or at Duck Lane Westminster, 'sought out a congregation by candle went into the lodging houses and got them to come and listen to the gospel'.[87] These were not conventional cottage pieties for they were part of the world which John Branch, the City Missionary, thus described to some of Mr. Hitchcock's young men – a world where 'men play cards over a corpse and another man coming home in a fit of intoxication and beating his wife with the dead body of an infant placed in a coffin in the house'.[88] Truth deprived this of melodrama.

Williams involved his friends in this world. In February 1844, he was at a Duck Lane lodging house with J. C. Symons. In September 1843 he, Valantine and the Cuttings had attended the 'Out door preaching at Paddington Station'. The preacher, Mr. Hinde ('a splendid sermon', a 'most powerful appeal') turned out to be an ex-draper from Valantine's midland haunts, and this encouraging encounter led to an invitation to call at Highbury College.[89]

Inevitably, this enthusiasm for home missions was accompanied by an equally incessant concern for foreign missions. Hitchcock, Rogers had intimate missionary links, so did the Weigh House and Craven Chapels. The mission field had a compelling romance for young men to whom emigration had become an attractive possibility. The London Missionary stood with the Church and Baptist Missionary Societies as the most prestigious of missionary agencies. The Colonial Missionary Society, with its particular concern for the West Indies, was of more recent origin (1836) but Thomas Binney had been a founding father. Indeed in both diaries the first entries for 1843 concern Robert Moffat, the almost legendary African pioneer, addressing a crowded hall of Sunday School children on African girls and boys.[90] Williams was the guiding spirit behind the missionary society which flourished at Hitchcock's, collecting its monies, apportioning them to the societies, and promoting local meetings. Concerning one of these, with its resolution of thankfulness for the work in the South Seas, the West Indies, India, Siberia, Africa, and China, he noted 'a consideration which had never before occupied the attention of Drapers so situated'.[91] The hint of self-congratulation was merited; so was Williams's subsequent discovery that he was collecting upwards of £20 a year for the cause.[92] 'Had our missionary tea in the Lecture room . . . abt 70 present', he wrote in December and Valantine, who estimated that 60 were there, added that the evening ended in song with 'Sound the loud timbrel'.[93]

It was the outside missionary meetings which were the great occasions. On Thursday, 11 May, Valantine's birthday and a holiday, the two friends enjoyed a field day. The L.M.S. annual meetings at the Exeter Hall were in the morning with Sir George Grey, M.P. in the chair and great pulpiteers massed round him. 'A nice meeting, but did not think it so good as last year', opined Williams; Valantine was less forthcoming – he sat at the back and heard little. In the evening there was a repeat performance at the Finsbury Chapel.[94] The following year the diet was varied, and on 30 May Williams, this time with his friends Angus and Beaumont, went to the missionary ship 'John Williams' and 'saw her over'. They then attended the ordination of a missionary to the South Seas where John Williams had so recently been martyred.[95]

Williams of Erromanga was a portentous figure for mission-conscious young men. He was already celebrated in countless Sunday Schools, and the memory of his friendship was now treasured by the moulders of his denomination. One of these was Andrew Reed, whose sermon for the L.M.S. of May 1831 had been regularly reprinted in subsequent years. Its peroration captured the appeal of it all:

'And still they are dying: now, while I speak – while you listen, they are dying! See how they pass along, melancholy, sad, and speechless, sinking down into endless night! Oh! If they would but stay till we could make one attempt for their salvation! No! they would, but they cannot; they are gone – they are gone! We shall meet them next in judgment. O Thou Judge of all, how shall we meet them? how shall we meet Thee, then?'[96]

Surely there were signs that Christianity was already overturning the world, even its uttermost ends. Where, in this, was the place of young men?

Notes

1. *Mss History*, n.d. (*c.* 1900) National Council MSS.
2. *Outlook*, 11 November 1905, (Selwyn Cuttings).
3. George Williams's *Diary*, Saturday, 4 February 1843.
4. ibid., Sunday, 31 December 1843; 27 November 1844; 21 December 1844.
5. ibid., Wednesday, 8 November 1844; December 1844.
6. Edward Valantine's *Diary*, Monday, 2 January 1843; Sunday, 8 January 1843; 20 January 1843; 11 January 1843.
7. ibid., 9 March 1843; 10 March 1843.
8. ibid., Tuesday, 23 May 1843; Williams's *Diary*, 24 May 1843.
9. Valantine's *Diary*, Wednesday, 11 October 1843.
10. Williams's *Diary*, 19 January 1843. Brother Robert was ten years older than George.
11. ibid., 8 April 1843.
12. ibid., June 1844.
13. Valantine's *Diary, passim* esp. 1–21 August 1844.
14. ibid., 26–7 June 1843.
15. ibid., 12 June 1844.
16. ibid., Saturday, 13 January 1844.
17. ibid., 25 February 1843; 5–8 April 1843.
18. ibid., Friday, 1 September 1843. On that day the shop first shut for winter at 8 p.m.
19. ibid., 9 October 1844; 18 October 1844.
20. Williams's *Diary*, 2 January 1843; 6 January 1843; 21 January 1843.
21. ibid., Monday, 16 January 1843; 30 January 1843; 25 February 1843; 9–10 June 1843; Tuesday, 1 September 1843; Monday, 15 March (?) 1844.
22. ibid., 4 January 1843.
23. ibid., 27 November 1844.
24. Quoted in J. T. Massey, *The Y.M.C.A. in Australia: A History*, (Melbourne, 1950) p. 19.
25. Diana Holman-Hunt, *My Grandfather, His Wives and Loves*, 1969, pp. 34–7.
26. Williams's *Diary*, Tuesday, 16 July; 17–21 July; 1 August 1844.
27. T. G. Bonney, *Memories of a Long Life*, (Cambridge, 1921) p. 2.
28. Williams's *Diary*, 23 March 1843; 29 December 1843. Valantine's *Diary*, 20 January 1844.
29. Valantine's *Diary*, 18 July 1844.
30. ibid., 31 January 1844; Monday, 28 October 1844.

31. ibid., Friday, 23 June 1843; Wednesday, 12 July 1843; Saturday, 27 April 1844.

32. ibid., 14 April 1843; Williams's *Diary*, 14 April 1843; for James Silk Buckingham 1786–1855 see *Dictionary of National Biography*.

33. Valantine's *Diary*, 15 March 1843.

34. A. and C. Reed, *Memoirs of . . . Andrew Reed D.D.*, 1863, pp. 130 et seq.

35. ibid., pp. 135 et seq. pp. 140–1.

36. ibid., pp. 237–9.

37. ibid., p. 205.

38. ibid., p. 212.

39. ibid., p. 204, p. 209; C. E. B. Reed, *Memoir of Sir Charles Reed*, 1883, pp. 19, 59–61.

40. A. and C. Reed op. cit., p. 209; Valantine's *Diary*, 16 April 1843; 26 March 1843.

41. A. and C. Reed op. cit., p. 214; C. E. B. Reed op. cit., p. 61; for Ainslie see below, note 53.

42. Williams's *Diary*, 11 June 1843; 10 May 1843; Valantine's *Diary*, 10 May 1843.

43. Williams's *Diary*, 12 May 1843; 17 August 1843.

44. Valantine's *Diary*, Sunday, 14 July 1844.

45. Williams's *Diary*, Thursday, 23 March 1843.

46. Williams's *Diary*, Thursday, 16 November 1843; Valantine's *Diary*, Wednesday, 22 November 1843.

47. G. Grove, 'John Hullah', *A Dictionary of Music and Musicians*, vol. 1, 1900, pp. 755–6; for John Curwen see *Dictionary of National Biography* and *Congregational Year Book*, 1881, pp. 336–9.

48. Williams's *Diary*, 13 January 1843; 17 January 1843; 20 January 1843; 23 January 1843; 3 February 1843. Valantine's *Diary*, 13 January 1843; 24 January 1843; 26 January 1843; 27 January 1843; 31 January 1843; 2 February 1843; 16 February 1843; 18 February 1843; 21 February 1843.

49. C. M. Davies, *Orthodox London*, Series I, 1873, p. 248.

50. Williams's *Diary*, November 1843; Valantine's *Diary*, 4 November 1843.

51. Valantine's *Diary*, 6 December 1843; Wednesday, 19 October 1844.

52. ibid., 13 December 1843; 7 February 1844.

53. Williams's *Diary*, 15 November 1843; Valantine's *Diary*, 15 November 1843; for Ainslie see *Transactions Unitarian Historical Society* 10, pp. 153–4; J. Campbell *Memoirs of David Nasmith*, 1844, pp. 331–8, 453. I am indebted for further information to the Revd. Duncan M. Whyte, General Secretary to the London City Mission.

54. Williams's *Diary*, 27 December 1843; 17 January 1844; 24 January 1844; Valantine's *Diary*, 3 January 1844.

55. Valantine's *Diary*, Friday, 5 January 1844.
56. J. E. Hodder Williams, *The Life of Sir George Williams*, 1906, p. 41.
57. Valantine's *Diary*, 11 June 1843; 20 August 1843.
58. ibid., 6 January 1843; 12 May 1844.
59. ibid., 5 March 1843.
60. ibid., 7 March 1843.
61. ibid., 21 March; 7 May 1843.
62. ibid., 15 October 1843.
63. ibid., 22 November 1843; 28 November 1843; 2 January 1844; Williams's *Diary*, 2 January 1844.
64. Williams's *Diary*, Tuesday, 31 January 1843.
65. ibid., 21 January 1843; 24 June 1843; Monday, 25 December 1843; Valantine's *Diary*, 25 December 1843.
66. Williams's *Diary*, 1 January 1843; 9 July 1843.
67. E. Paxton Hood, *Thomas Binney: His Mind, Life and Opinions*, 1874, p. 49; Valantine's *Diary*, 1 October 1843.
68. Valantine's *Diary*, 5 February 1843.
69. Williams's *Diary*, 1 March 1843.
70. Valantine's *Diary*, 12 February 1843; 23 April 1843; 30 April 1843; 28 May 1843; 10 December 1843.
71. King's Weigh House Domestic Mission, *Committee Meeting Minutes 1842–54*; King's Weigh House Domestic Mission *Annual Reports*, 1854 and 1855 *passim*.
72. Elaine Kaye, *The History of the King's Weigh House Church*, 1968, pp. 91 et seq.
73. Williams's *Diary*, 22 January 1843; 29 January 1843.
74. Valantine's *Diary*, 9 January 1843; 6 March 1843; Williams's *Diary*, 12 March 1843.
75. Valantine's *Diary*, Sunday, 21 May 1843; Williams's *Diary*, Sunday, 20 [sic] May 1843.
76. See Southwark Sunday School Society, *Minute Book*, 1816–1821; Southwark Sunday School Society, *Sheet Report*, 1836; *Annual Address of the Committee of the Southwark Sunday School Society*, February 1841, p. 5; *Annual Address of the Committee of the Southwark Sunday School Society*, February 1845, p. 5; J. W. Read (ed.) *The Christ Church Souvenir Jubilee Book*, 1926, pp. 53–4 (in the possession of Christ Church and Upton Chapel, Westminster Bridge Road, London).
77. Valantine's *Diary*, 4 February 1844.
78. ibid., 28 April 1844.
79. *Annual Address of the Committee of the Southwark Sunday School Society*, 1845, p. 5; Southwark Sunday School Society, *Minute Book*, 1828–1845 *passim*.

80. Surrey Chapel Sunday School, *Memoir Book*; Southwark Sunday School Society, *Minute Book*, 1799–1815.

81. For Cranfield 1758–1838 see (R. Cranfield), *Memoir of Thomas Cranfield* by His Son, n.d. (*c.* 1840).

82. *Annual Address of the Committee of the Southwark Sunday School Society*, February 1845, p. 8.

83. A. and C. Reed, op. cit., p. 20.

84. ibid.

85. Cranfield, op. cit., p. 259.

86. A. and C. Reed, op. cit., p. 26; C. E. B. Reed, op. cit., p. 31.

87. Williams's *Diary*, Monday, 30 January 1843; Sunday, 19 March 1843; 20 May 1843 (when, that evening, Williams heard a 'solemn' Leifchild on the Second Advent and Valantine returned to hear Binney on Sodom and Gomorrah); 25 June 1843; 12 November 1843.

88. Valantine's *Diary*, 9 October 1843.

89. Williams's *Diary*, 4 February 1844; Valantine's *Diary*, 3 September 1843.

90. Williams's *Diary*, 1 January 1843; 7 January 1843; Valantine's *Diary*, 1 January 1843.

91. Williams's *Diary*, 24 May 1843.

92. ibid., 18 November 1843.

93. ibid., 15 December 1843; Valantine's *Diary*, 15 December 1843.

94. Valantine's *Diary*, 11 May 1843; Williams's *Diary*, 10 [*sic*] May 1843.

95. In 1839. Williams's *Diary*, 30 May 1844.

96. A. and C. Reed, op. cit., p. 267.

CHAPTER VI

6 June 1844

In August 1845 George Williams wrote to his friend William Creese, who was now in Worcestershire, his home county:

'My Dear Old Brother Creese

No doubt it is for the best but I miss you very much – I want to see your old smiling face, but (?) is well – yes all well – "even so Father" – "let thy will be done, anything" – I hope your peace abounds sometimes mine is almost gone but hope now to begin afresh. had a very delightful meeting with the young xtns last evening in our room.

We are thinking of having something like a class meeting among them that is for them to relate any particular trial and temptation that besets them –

I hope they are getting on pretty well –

Do pray for us. Symons is returned from the country and I hope happier in God which is a very great mercy. I had indeed a hallowed and stirring time home – Oh, *shout* God is at work I have numbers under conscern (?) and asking the way to Sion –

Mr. Creese cry aloud to the people where you dwell and God will be with you with all the love of my heart

I am still

Your old Frd and Brother

Geo Williams'.[1]

This letter, 'written in bedroom at St. Pauls Chyard at ½ past 8; Tuesday morning', does more than demonstrate the incoherence which often marked George Williams's outward expression, for it shows the abundant geniality which impressed all who met him. There was a genuineness about him which transcended other qualities. Without this the atmosphere at St. Paul's Churchyard would have been intolerable. With it, the activities of the first Christian Young Men became natural, even unremarkable, and entirely acceptable. There was, moreover, a persistence about Williams which only a strong character and formed intelligence could resist. The young man was manifestly good at his job and he was no fool, despite the crevices in his intellectual armoury. From the first his ability in harnessing, utilizing and keeping the abilities of more articulate men, and better organizers or greater men of the world, is striking. This was partly the good businessman's ability to delegate authority without abdicating responsibility. Partly it was an extension of the good draper's sixth sense – an ability to sum up and mentally to clothe his fellow men. It was certainly the one thing needful to transmute the activities at No. 72, St. Paul's Churchyard into a Young Men's Christian Association.

The ground was ready for this. To what extent a pattern was consciously emerging is harder to decide. It seemed sensible to later generations, and to the founders grown old and marvelling at the results of their work, to assume that some particular agency was at work in a recognizable way. The 1840s were, in retrospect, a decade notable for movement. William Creese remained impressed with the part played by Finney's books, and much later William Hind Smith asserted that the 'intense earnestness' engendered by such study led to the sort of 'allotment plan' which was undoubtedly in vogue amongst other groups. There were five steps – each Young Man first assumed a special care for certain unconverted friends. He would then regularly and by name pray for each one. He would speak to them on serious matters, he would persuade them to accompany him to church. He would urge them to sample the prayer meeting or a Bible study group.[2] Such a system makes sense of aspects of Williams's diary; there was something businesslike in it, at once quite rational and wholly Evangelical. Yet no system, least of all one involving 'soul welfare', can work unless the personalities concerned are sympathetic as well as powerful. It might have required a system to make Williams abstain from gluttony or jump earlier out of bed. It needed no such thing to make him deeply anxious for his fellows.

With this qualification, it is possible to see a development in intensity and spiritual awareness (which is not quite the same thing) amongst the Christians at Hitchcock, Rogers. It started in 1843, perhaps earlier. It reached a peak in the summer of 1844. Amidst the depression which was so frequent in the diaries, and which came as strongly in mid-1844 as in early 1843, there was also a growing, and moving, realization that their strivings after usefulness were bearing fruit. They achieved what is denied to many maturer Christians. They could have had no stronger sign of the truth of their faith and the certainty of its ultimate victory.

By the early spring of 1843 the Christian work at Hitchcock's was established and it was more than capable of silencing opposition. Mr. Hitchcock himself was well-disposed and the Christian young men were at once too widely-spread and too closely-knit to fall back. But they could not afford to sit on their laurels. There was a perpetual coming and going among the assistants and the temptations of the City hardly lessened. There was now a most exhilarating edge to their lives of Christian usefulness.

By the end of March this was being turned to account. For Williams it was outwardly a busy, profitable time; inwardly he felt it to be dark. On Wednesday the 28th he noted: 'nice prayer meeting in the evening 14 attended'. The following night, in the midst of being 'much occupied with the world', Valantine wrote: 'I and Brother Williams has set apart for prayer to the intent that God would pour out his spirit upon us and make us more desirous after the welfare of others.' And at the end of the week Brother Williams found 'much to encourage . . . as many young hands has entered amongst whom we have been enabled to break the bread of life'.[3] The Wednesday prayer meeting at Hitchcock's may always have been intended for 'the conversion of the young men' – by May 1843 it certainly was.[4] There was now an urgency about it. At the May Meetings of the Missionary Societies, Williams was particularly convinced of his duty to act yet more strenuously in spreading the gospel on home ground.[5] This was at the very time that he was increasingly involved with visiting cottages for Craven Chapel, and in turning the attention of No. 72's Missionary Society to the cause of home missions, and in ensuring that Brother Valantine thought with him.

By now the connexions were accumulating. On 4 June, with Edward Valantine, Edward Beaumont and three others, Williams went to hear Dr. Leifchild's annual sermon to Young Men. He found it 'a powerful discourse'.[6] The agencies within Hitchcock's were proliferating – twenty were coming to the Bible Class. On the last day of the month a fresh prayer meeting was started in No. 1 Sitting Room. It met for an hour, and fourteen attended.[7]

At this point two outside, but connected, agencies intervened. They need mention here although their fuller significance must be considered later. The first was the conversion of Mr. Hitchcock himself. The importance of this was that his influence combined with his sympathy could lift any movement among his assistants on to a permanent level. This became clear in August, while George Williams was on holiday in Dulverton. Valantine recorded it, 'all of us informed by Mr. Hitchcock this p.m. that family prayer would in future be carried on in the establishment every morning at 7 o'clock what I hope through the blessing of God will prove beneficial to the souls of all in the House'. That was on Saturday, 13 August. On the following Monday the 'Family Prayer' began, 'a Gent of the name of Branch officiating'.[8] George Williams encountered him three weeks later: 'Mr. Branch a very delightful man,' he noted approvingly.[9]

John Branch was ideally suited to his post. He was a Baptist. Since 1839 he had been a London City Missionary serving in the Coram Street district. In 1840 a proposal that he be appointed missionary to the theatre land of Covent Garden and Drury Lane under the patronage of William Cowper, M.P., Lord Ashley's brother-in-law, failed to be implemented but it suggested vigour and aggressiveness in him. In September 1842, Branch became general superintendent of the City Missionaries.[10] Doubtless his appointment at Hitchcock's was a welcome addition to his arduous and miserably paid calling,* but he made far more of it than serving as a mere morning minister. In a real sense he became chaplain to the house, appearing with his wife at its functions and entertaining the young men at his own home on Monday evenings. Branch appears in the diaries as a man who was at once serious and companionable, deserving the affection and respect of his flock, a man, moreover, whose faith was mature and who used it to guide the young men into fruitful, outward-looking paths. The Y.M.C.A. owes him a profound debt.

On 2 October Williams noted: 'went with 8 other of the brethren to Mr. Branches for mutual improvement'. Valantine communicates

---

* Williams's *Diary*, 1 September 1843. His initial salary in 1839 was £70 p.a. It is not clear what he received from Hitchcock. In January 1844 the London City Mission disallowed a request by Hitchcock to pay Branch a separate salary and Hitchcock instead agreed to make a contribution to Mission funds.

a little of the primness of it: '. . . had some truly instructive conversation touching upon the necessity of working for Christ amongst the young men of this Establishment. . . .'[11] The instances multiply – 'an especiall meeting for the purpose of beseeching Almighty God to outpour his spirit upon us'. That was on the following Saturday and on the Tuesday next the prayer seemed to be answered – there were twenty-five at the Bible Class in No. 2.[12] The prayer meetings 'especially for the young men' continued throughout the winter. So did more intimate occasions as when Williams, Valantine, Creese, and three others had supper together in No. 2 on one of their usual prayer evenings.[13] Beyond this there is perhaps only one entry for 1843 which is worthy of further note. On Friday, 17 November after the usual prayer meeting a further one '$\frac{1}{2}$ an hour long' was established 'for the young xtns to engage'.[14] Williams was already held in the power of prayer – how important for newly-awakened men to practise it openly and without embarrassment.

The year 1844 broke characteristically for Williams and Valantine. Valantine heard Bow Bells while he was at prayer, and then the bell of St. Paul's brought to mind 'solemn recollections of sins committed talents misinformed time trifled away. . . .' George Williams, with less sense of occasion, was up and doing. He went to a tea and he attended a Wesleyan Class Meeting. Many of the meetings at Hitchcock's resembled a Methodist Class Meeting and the resemblance was probably a conscious one. He 'enjoyed it much'.[15]

So the year's activities began. They were more numerous, they were attacked with more assured zeal, but they were not different in kind. In February, however, an event occurred which brought home to them all the transience of even their reborn lives. Amidst the sore throats and colds natural to the season, a more serious illness appeared. Several were affected and one, 'Poor Morse', died. Rheumatic fever had affected his heart. 'Poor fellow he was called away I am afraid unprepared.' Aware of this awful circumstance they held a prayer meeting. Williams laconically sets the scene, 'Poor Morse died a state of consternation had a prayer meeting in sitting room.' As usual Valantine expands this, noting incidentally that the meeting was in the library. Brother 'Symmons' presided, Brother Williams engaged with him in prayer. So did Brother 'Crese'. Poor Brother Smith was so overcome that he was forced to sit down. There was an address, they sang hymns, 'nearly all were moved to tears the coffin having just been taken through the room before the service began.'[16]

Death was common enough for men in their position, but poor Morse had died before he reached material prosperity and without hope of spiritual prosperity. He had died in a house of Christian Young Men. Those who arranged the service were all founder members of the Y.M.C.A. and they could not fail to improve upon such an opportunity. They were also intimate friends. In an atmosphere where privacy was impossible, it seems hard to overestimate the effect of Morse's death.

The funeral was on the 18th, a Sunday. It was a simple affair, six going in a coach and twenty on foot to Nunhead Cemetery. Poor Valentine did not go. He was in a muddled state, 'Oh Lord thou hast taken him to thyself and yet the thought seems to contradict my desire when I think the life he led.' Williams went. He much enjoyed the walk.[17]

From now on Williams's diary becomes fragmentary and disorganized. It is Valentine who tells of the continuing meetings on 'The young man's answer to Christ.'[18] The absence of entries might in itself be a sign of Williams's consciousness that great work is to be done and at once. Almost certainly the next important entry (which he misdates to 30 June 1844 – he means May) indicates this. Its tone proclaims excitement and expectancy, 'Many young men under deep conviction Rogers Crisp Beaumont last night had a solemn meeting on the outpouring of the Spirit. God seems about to send his Holy Spirit and this to turn sinners from the errors of their ways –'*

The reference to Rogers and Beaumont carries us to the heart of the spiritual excitement which was now so marked at No. 72. For Edward Beaumont in particular this was a time which was not to be forgotten – he experienced conversion. As usual, Edward Valantine describes it. On Monday, 20 May he wrote briefly, 'E. Beaumont not in the shop unwell.' The next day he explained this. Beaumont's absence was due to rather more than a sudden indisposition. 'This day E.B. in the shop as usual evidently the spirit of God striving with him in answer to the prayers offered up at the throne of grace. Bible class this evening. E.B. present appearing very much affectd pour a spirit O Lord carry on the work we beseech thee and lead him to repentance and the forsaking of his sins adopt him into thy family and enable him to come along with us.'[19]

May was a stirring month for Evangelical Christians, and for

* It must be between 20 and 30 May; 30 May would make most sense. There is no evidence that Rogers was related to Hitchcock's late partner.

Congregationalists the new missionary ship 'John Williams' and the ordination of missionaries to those South Sea Islands where John Williams had so recently been martyred, were especially exciting. Hitchcock, Rogers moreover were busy with missionary orders, a practical reminder that the principal's three sisters were married to missionaries, two of them in the South Seas, and of John Williams's own dictum that 'at the lowest computation, a hundred and fifty or two hundred thousand persons, who a few years ago were unclothed savages, are now wearing and using articles of British manufacture'.[20] All these concerns were close to George Williams's heart and now that Beaumont was experiencing transformation in his life, he too was drawn closer to Williams. There was a mingling of mission.

On 30 May, as has been seen,* the two of them accompanied Brother Angus to 'see over' the missionary ship. That was in the course of a week without parallel in their inner lives. On Sunday 26 May, a day whose services were full of missionary interest, Valantine had noted, 'E.B.G.W. at Chapel'. He does not say which chapel, presumably it was the Weigh House.[21] In the evening they were again 'at chapel'. Edward Beaumont recalled it fifteen years later, in a letter to George Williams. The origins of the Y.M.C.A. were already matters of controversy, and Beaumont felt that he was uniquely placed to recall what really had happened. Like Williams, he had prospered in trade, and his City Drapery Stores were most eligibly placed in the Oxford High. Beaumont had moreover married a former saleswoman of Mr. Holmes's in Bridgwater and he was a pillar of Oxford Congregationalism.† The date of his spiritual rebirth was 26 May 1844; how could he forget any event associated with those days?

> 'On one Sunday evening in the latter end of May 1844 you accompanied me to Surry [*sic*.] Chapel to hear my dear pastor the Revd. James Sherman preach – after walking a few moments in silence you said pressing my arm and addressing me familiarly as you were in the habit of doing – "Teddy are you prepared to make a sacrifice for Christ?" I replied: "if call'd upon to do so I think and hope I can." You then told me that you had been deeply impress'd with the importance of introducing religious services

---

* See Chapter V, p. 105.
† The premises, 10-12 High Street, are now C. P. Webber's. See also J. E. Hodder Williams, *The Life of George Williams*, 1906, p. 22.

such as we enjoyed at 72 St. Pauls into every large establishment
in London, and that you thought that if a few earnest devoted and
self denying men could be found to unite themselves together for
this purpose that with earnest prayer God would smile upon the
effort and much may be done – I need not say that I heartily
concurred and said I would gladly do what I could to assist you –
you told me at the same time that I was the only person to whom
you had mentioned it.'[22]

The whole of the journey to and from the Surrey Chapel, which lay
south of the river over the Blackfriars Bridge, was taken up with
the matter.

The events of the next few days intensified this determination.
On Wednesday, 29, the day before Beaumont visited the missionary
ship, Edward Valantine felt strangely moved. 'I began with greater
love to God than usual.' The business of the day was in the dispatch
of the house's missionary orders, then 'G. Wms. came and said he
believ'd something particular was going to take place today inasmuch
as the spirit's operation seemed visible in our midst a young man of
the name of Rogers [first Beaumont, now Rogers: there remained
only Crisp] was seriously impressed about his soul's salvation.'
Williams was with Rogers at this time and Mr. Hitchcock showed
sympathy. It was decided to hold a prayer meeting that evening

'. . . and whilst engaged packing up a parcel Rogers came to me
and told me that he was thinking something very seriously about
his immortal soul having previously opposed us by the conduct
he had manifested. I spoke some encouraging passages and told
him to hope in Christ to throw himself upon him and accept his
salvation, at 9. o'clock we assembled for an especial outpouring
of the Holy Spirit upon the unconverted of the house as also the
blessing of God to rest on those who had felt the burden of sin
and a solemn meeting it was a great number were there I open'd
the meeting after a Hymn had been sung with prayer. I felt more
than ever the necessity of pleading for the spirit's operation upon
the hearts of the unconverted.'

The service was held in No. 10. There were hymns, and Williams,
Creese and Symons all led in prayer.[23]

The conversion of Rogers was a famous victory and from it comes
the story of the oyster supper which has enlivened Y.M.C.A. lore.[24]

There had developed a prayerful battle between Williams and Rogers, whose conviviality accompanied an undisguised contempt for the Christian young men. But it was his conviviality which opened Rogers to salvation. The Christians in the house, hiding all thoughts of overt conversion, invited him to an oyster supper. As payment for his enjoyment he went to one of their meetings and thus frivolity was sanctified. It all underlined the ripeness of the time for more concerted action and, so Beaumont recalled, it was after one of the week's meetings when a few 'of the religious men' had lingered behind, that Williams elaborated his concern for further work. They decided 'to call a meeting of all the religious young men of the House'; which was to be on Thursday, 6 June and it was to discuss the formation of a more widely-based association.[25]

Again, outside agencies intervened at this point. On Sunday, 2 June, which was Ordinance Sunday at the Weigh House, Valantine 'with several others' went in the evening to the Craven Chapel. Dr. Leifchild was preaching his annual sermon to Young Men. His text was 'I gave my heart to know wisdom' and what he said was 'most impressive'.[26]

At the same time the conviction which now dominated the young men at Hitchcock's was being shared in other business houses, most notably at Mr. Owen's of 44 Great Coram Street. W. D. Owen was acquainted with George Hitchcock. He was a man of similar outlook and vigour, a draper, a pioneer of Ragged School work in London, and of the Early Closing Movement. Owen must have been acquainted with John Branch, who had worked in Coram Street in 1839. With George Hitchcock, Owen was the Y.M.C.A's earliest influential lay supporter and some persisted in regarding him as the Association's father, if not godfather.

It is not easy to discover the exact part Owen and his lieutenant, James Smith, played in the formation of the Y.M.C.A. Most sources of information date from years after the event and depend on reminiscence. Edward Beaumont recalled that some days before 6 June, in the course of a visit to Hitchcock's, Owen and Williams talked together 'and on your telling him what we contemplated doing on the following Thursday Mr. Owen said it was a remarkable thing that the same subject had been occupying his thoughts and that he hoped something for the spiritual improvement of young men may be accomplished – he also said he would send Mr. Smith one of his young men who was an excellent Christian and I think Deacon of a

Christian Church to consult with and assist us at our meeting – on the 6th June, 1844 we met . . .'[27]

W. E. Shipton, that formidable statesman of the Association, considered that Owen's man Smith was already conducting similar meetings at Owen's. Shipton contended that when Owen heard of the movement afoot in St. Paul's Churchyard he told Smith, whereupon a letter was dispatched to Hitchcock's on 31 May. That same evening, so Williams replied, his friends were meeting to discuss prayer meetings in other City houses.[28] This must be the meeting of a few 'religious men' mentioned in Beaumont's letter as leading to the decisive meeting of 6 June. Shipton's accounts are stamped with authority and most subsequent narratives rely heavily upon them, sometimes tying the ends rather too tidily. R. R. McBurney, for example, argued that Owen had learned of Hitchcock's young men at the time of Hitchcock's own spiritual decision. This encounter led to James Smith setting up prayer meetings at Owen's on his principal's advice, and then writing to Williams:

'I have been truly rejoiced to hear that the Lord is doing a great work in your house. . . . I am engaged here in the same work, but stand almost alone; and, from what I have heard, am induced to say, "come over and help us." We have a prayer-meeting this evening at half-past eight. Mr. Branch will be with us. Will you oblige us by your company? and, if you can bring a praying brother with you, do. If you could by any possibility be here at eight, I should be glad; as I want to advise with you on another subject in reference to our trade, viz: whether anything can be done in other houses.'[29]

Williams, with or without the 'praying brother', attended, and the following Thursday, which was 6 June, a similar meeting was held this time at Hitchcock's.

What actually happened on that occasion is shrouded in mystery and contradiction and it gave rise to loving controversy. Williams's diary is at once reticent and surprising, 'Beaumont Rogers and Crisp getting on nicely – myself not enjoying so much of hallow communion.'[30] That is all. Valantine is his usual more informative self, 'Thursday 6. Met in G. Williams room for the purpose of forming a society the object of which is to influence young men (Religious) to spread the Redeemer's Kingdom amongst those by whom they are surrounded. Mr. Smith of Coram St. President self Treasurer

Brothers Crese Symons Secretaries, Committee those then present belonging to us'.[31] But who were 'those then present belonging to us'? There is one almost conclusive piece of evidence, and there is an abundance of legend. The piece of evidence is a copy of a minute taken at the meeting by Edward Valantine:

> 'At a meeting held in No. 14 for purpose of establishing a society which should have for its object the arousing of converted men in the different drapery Establishments in the Metropolis to a sense of their obligation and responsibility as Christians in diffusing religious knowledge to those around them either through the medium of prayer meetings or any other meetings they think proper the following individuals were elected to take office for the present with power to add to the members Mr. Smith (Gt. Coram St.) Vice President
>
>
>
> Valantine   –   –   Treasurer
>
> Secretaries
>
> Messrs Symons, Williams*, Crese
>
> Comittee of Management
>
> Williams, Benton, Beaumont, Rogers, Glasson,
>
> Owen Harvey Cockett & Smith
>
>
> Meeting for the present weekly every Thursday Evening Commenced and closed with prayer.
>
> Monies collected – 13/-
>
> June 6th, 1844.
>
> Treasurer Valantine.'[32]
>
> [*Author's note: *Williams crossed through in original*]

It is here that confusion begins. Valantine gives thirteen names, so, some fifteen years later ('but I have no memmorandum') did Edward Beaumont, save that Beaumont replaced Benton with the third Smith (Norton Smith) and he commented that 'Wm. Owen a son of Mr. Owen's an interesting lad who was living at 72 and who slept in this same room with you was also present but of course took no part in its deliberations.'† In this way Beaumont could make his recollection, which time had telescoped in other respects, square with the generally

---

† E. Beaumont to G. Williams, 22 October 1859(?) (copy Nat. Counc. MSS.). The three Smiths are confusing. James Smith fades from the scene; C. W. Smith, originator of the name Y.M.C.A., is the most frequently mentioned in the diaries. Norton Smith survived to be among the founder members gracing the platforms of the Golden Jubilee.